Praise for *Less*

*This organizing minimalist knows what she has, what she doesn't have, what she wants, and what she doesn't need. She's a real role model. Everyone can learn **Less** from Rose Lounsbury. Buy this book (and, hey, pass it on).*

— Dorothy The Organizer, Expert Organizer,
A&E TV show "Hoarders"

Read the first few pages of this book and you'll be hooked. I loved the real life examples and solutions that Rose Lounsbury offers on the path to minimalism. If your things leave you with less time for yourself and you secretly wish that your life would be less hectic and stressful, this eye-opening book is for you.

— Stephanie Culp, author of the bestselling
How to Conquer Clutter

I need this. When you're a clutterer like me, you don't even have a system to unclutter. This gives you a step-by-step guide. I love it!

— Dr. Will Miller, author of *Miserable@Work: Stop Blaming the Job and Fix What's Really Broken*

Brilliant!

— Ericka Young, financial coach and author of *Naked and Unashamed: 10 Money Conversations Every Couple Must Have*

Less

Minimalism for Real

Practical Ways to Live
Better by Owning Less

Less

Minimalism for Real

Practical Ways to Live
Better by Owning Less

ROSE LOUNSBURY

Niche Pressworks

Indianapolis, IN

Less. Minimalism, For Real

Copyright © 2017 Rose Lounsbury

Printed in the United States of America

Published by Niche Pressworks

P.O. Box 80031

Indianapolis, IN 46280

NichePressworks.com

ISBN: 978-1-946533-17-3

Library of Congress Control Number: 2017912595

Dedication

To Josh, Orlando, Mercedes and Reese,
where everything important begins and ends.

Acknowledgements

I would like to thank every teacher who ever encouraged me to write or to believe in myself, especially Mrs. Pasant, Mrs. Green, Mrs. Maharg, Mr. Smigell, Mrs. Commire, Mr. Meck, Shanda, and most importantly, my mom and dad. Good teachers are the best people in the world, and I would not be the person I am today without your time, energy, and love.

To the amazing folks at the Ohio Writing Project, thank you for teaching me everything I know about this slippery task called writing.

To Megan, Breana, and Grandma Gin, thank you for graciously watching my children so I could write this book. And I hope you weren't lying when you said they were well-behaved.

To my awesome publishers, Nicole "Feather Rising" Gebhardt and Crystal "Travel Delay" Yeagy. I always wondered why people thanked their publishers when they wrote a book and now I get it. Writing a book is like birthing a baby and you two were my loyal midwives, encouraging me to keep pushing. (And I will stop with that metaphor right now. You're all welcome.)

To my fellow organizing and productivity folks who graciously shared their understanding of RAFT with me: Julie Bestry, Lisa Montanero, Anne Langton, and Charlie Gilkey. I say we all don superhero capes and unite to banish paper piles forever!

To my dear blog readers and cheerleaders, thank you for your continual support and encouragement. A writer is not a writer without readers. I am deeply indebted to your precious time and eyeballs.

And mostly, thank you to Josh, who stands beside me every day of this crazy life and tells me I'm beautiful.

Table of Contents

Preface

Five years ago, I lived the very busy life of a full-time working mother with 3-year-old triplets. If that sentence alone doesn't make you feel exhausted, here's a more detailed look at my daily schedule:

6:00am: Wake up, shower, and eat breakfast under cover of darkness in the hopes of escaping my house before the kids wake up. (Because after that, they're the nanny's job.)

6:45am: Quietly back car out of driveway, headlights off, just as I hear the first whimper of awakening children. Whew. Made it.

7:00am: Arrive at school. For the next seven hours, do my darndest to instill the values of Language Arts to 150 7th graders.

3:30pm: Clock in at job #2: Mom to 3-year-old triplets. For the next five hours, do my darndest not to lose my patience and/or pass out from sheer exhaustion.

4:00pm: Trip to the park. Only one tantrum about the choice of sand toys—we are making progress!

6:00pm: Dinner of macaroni and cheese. Because cheese is dairy and macaroni is grain, so we've got two food groups covered, right?

7:00pm: Bath time (aka "How wet can the bathroom floor get? Let's see!") followed by pajama time (aka "How much more fun is it to run around naked than to put these pajamas on? Lots!")

7:30pm: Arrival of Josh. Forced smile at his "Sorry-I'm-late-forgot-to-put-the-meeting-on-the-calendar" and hand him a wet, squirmy kid to wrangle into aforementioned pajamas.

7:45pm: Brush teeth. No, don't eat the toothpaste. It's poison. Just brush them. Like this. No, I'm not doing it for you. You're old enough now. What would the dentist say, huh? You want me to call Dr. Coyne right now? I have his number. I can call him anytime I want. (Grit teeth as I realize this is a ludicrous lie.) Just. Brush. Your. Teeth.

8:00pm: Stories. My mouth reads words about a red truck and a puppy while my brain cycles through various versions of, "I'm so tired, I am just so tired, why aren't they in bed yet? I just want them in bed …"

8:30pm: Goodnight kisses. I love you so, so much, but please, for the love of all that's holy, go to sleep.

8:45pm: Sigh. It's finally quiet.

8:50pm: Begin my evening routine: whirl around my house, picking up toys, sippy cups, shoes, books, and other miscellany. Stuff into already-overflowing bins. Re-arrange paper piles on my kitchen counter into what I perceive as neater-looking paper piles. Survey laundry situation in distress. Put laundry into washer and pray I remember to move it to the dryer. Pray harder that a troop of magical elves appears to fold and put it away.

9:30pm: Legs will no longer move willingly. Time for bed.

10:00pm: In bed. Try to keep eyes open long enough to read. (I love to read! Why, oh why, can't I ever *just read?*) Suddenly remember—darn it!—I didn't move the laundry to the dryer. Briefly weigh pros and cons of getting out of bed to do this. Opt to stay in bed, telling myself that I'll surely remember in the morning …

10:15pm: Pass out.

To say I was busy is a bit of an understatement. But for me, the hardest part was not teaching or taking care of three toddlers. I found both those jobs, while exhausting, ultimately rewarding. The part that never felt right was how I spent the precious time between my kids' bedtime and my own.

You see, while I'm quite friendly, I'm a natural introvert who needs alone time to recharge. Without it, I'm no good to anyone. I can tell when I haven't had enough personal time. I get irritated and actively avoid other people.

I'll duck down a different aisle in the grocery store to avoid running into an acquaintance or purposely not answer my phone when a friend calls. I'm not proud to admit that I do these things, but I know they are a direct result of not having enough time to *myself*.

And as you can see from my daily schedule, "me time" was in short supply.

A quick analysis of my day-in-the-life reveals the culprit: not my children or my students. The real problem was my stuff.

When I had time that I could have spent relaxing and recharging, I dealt with my things—frantically stuffing them away, trying to control the chaos that threatened to overtake my home.

This, ultimately, was the reason I was so exhausted at the end of the day. I spent my only unstructured time just trying to put my house back in order. I longed to sit on my couch, relaxing with a beverage, reading a novel. But that never happened.

Enter Minimalism

Around this time, I had a fateful lunch date with a good friend of mine, Robin. I realize that sounds a bit dramatic, but when I look back, I realize that this lunch changed everything.

It was a week after Christmas. We had just returned from visiting relatives, our van loaded with presents.

"I don't even have room in my house for the toys my kids already have," I told Robin. "How can I fit this stuff in there? Maybe I need a bigger house."

In fact, Josh and I had started looking at bigger homes. We lived in our 1,500-square foot "starter" home with not just our kids, but also a live-in nanny. We all felt the squeeze.

Robin listened calmly, as she always does, and then asked a question that changed my life:

"Have you ever thought about minimalism?"

This word—"minimalism"—was not familiar to me. I thought about Tibetan monks meditating in caves and white-walled art galleries with canvases that are painted all black. I could not see how any of that related to me.

"Uh," I stammered, trying to be polite. "Isn't that for, like, monks or something?"

Robin laughed and explained that anyone—even a suburban American mom, like myself—could adopt a minimalist lifestyle by simply choosing to own less. As we talked, I started to see how having less could make my life simpler and less stressful. At the end of our lunch, Robin pointed me to some books and blogs on the subject.

I went home and started reading. I was hooked.

Eight Months Later

"Whoa! What did you do in here? Are you guys moving?" my friend Dan's daughter, Becca, said as she walked in the door, taking in my newly decluttered and minimized living room.

I laughed.

"No," I said. "I just got rid of all the stuff we don't need. This is how it looks now."

Becca took a moment to survey the new, uncluttered surroundings.

"It looks good," she concluded.

I couldn't agree more.

Me Time

Becca was right. My house did look good, much better, in fact, than it had ever looked, even before I had kids. (And in case you're wondering, Josh and I had abandoned our search for the "bigger, better house" when we realized the simple difference minimalism made in our existing home.)

But for me, the best part of my "new" house wasn't how it looked. The best part was the re-emergence of my personal time.

Because now, at the end of those long days—which were still exhausting, filled with teaching and parenting—I had time to relax. I no longer spent that brief, precious window between bedtimes picking up toys and shoes.

Because as I decluttered my house, a slow truth dawned upon me: *When you have less stuff, you have more time.*

Less toys are more quickly put in their containers, less shoes are more easily paired and set by the door, less clothing is more quickly laundered and put away.

So where was I at the end of my days now?

On my couch, book in hand, enjoying a mug of tea.

I was free.

How a Blog Became a Business

Throughout the eight-month decluttering process, I kept a blog, chronicling my journey. I enjoyed the writing, but more importantly, it kept me accountable and focused on my goal. Decluttering an entire house—even one that is only 1,500 square feet—is no small task, and the positive comments from my readers kept me going.

After a while, some of those reader comments became requests for help in their own homes. My pulse beat excitedly at the thought of digging into someone else's cluttered closets (yes, I know this is strange!), but I was bound by my teaching career and young family, and couldn't see how my blogging hobby could become an actual career.

Yet this, in and of itself, is another benefit of minimalism. As the excess stuff slowly left my house and I had more time to listen to myself, I realized that teaching full-time was not the right path for me. My kids were now about four years old and better able to express themselves. Phrases like, "I want tomorrow to be a mama day," squeezed my heart. Particularly painful was my kids' preschool holiday program, when I introduced myself to one of the teachers and she said, "Oh, *you're* the mom."

Don't get me wrong. I believe in the power of working women. And I don't believe in changing careers because of guilt or any other negative emotion. But I do believe in listening to my gut—it has never steered me wrong.

Because I had let go of many of my possessions, my life was simpler. I had time to focus and think. And with my newfound reflective time, one particular thought kept cropping up in my mind: *My kids are too young for me to not be more present in their lives.*

I knew that if I could rework my professional life to be more available to my family, that would be a good thing.

So, I took a leap. I left teaching and opened shop as a minimalism and simplicity coach. Because I believe, very personally, that creating more open spaces in your home is at the heart of significant life change.

Why I Wrote this Book

I wrote this book to share how minimalism has impacted my life, and to encourage you to consider giving it a try. If you feel overwhelmed by clutter in your home or workspace, or if you just feel distracted and like something is "not quite right" in your life, I encourage you to read on.

Minimalism is a simple philosophy. But, as I have found in my own life, it can have powerful effects.

I hope you choose to join me.

Introduction

This is a book of my stories. Everything I share is based on my own experience as someone who has not only adopted minimalism, but also has worked with others to help them achieve their minimalist goals.

Minimalism is relative. What minimalism looks like to me is not what it looks like to my individual clients, and it will not be what it looks like for you. That's okay. I've read articles about minimalism that suggest discarding a certain number or type of items. I've also heard of minimalists who can fit all their possessions into a backpack or duffel bag.

While these approaches certainly have their merit, this is not a one-size-fits-all kind of book. My goal is to provide a realistic approach to minimalism, one that is based solidly in my own experience and that allows readers to shape minimalism into something that works for them.

The goal of minimalism is to live a simpler, more purposeful life, a life that aligns more closely with your values. Minimalism eliminates that clutter—physical and otherwise—that distracts us from what truly matters.

As you read this book, we will move from some background on minimalism—focusing on the benefits of this lifestyle and how to adopt a minimalist mindset—into more specific how-to's and examples of how minimalism looks in my life and the lives of my clients. I will also address some tricky issues when it comes to minimalism, such as how to deal with paper, memorabilia, and gifts. I hope you find it helpful, humorous, and most of all, inspiring.

Thank you for joining me on this journey. Exciting life changes await!

CHAPTER 1

The Joy of Open Space

I've been an on-and-off insomniac for much of my adult life. It started my first year of teaching, when I spent nights anxiously rewriting lesson plans in my head, trying to create the most whiz-bang learning experience of my students' lives.

Little did I know, at that time, that seventh-graders do not consider English class the most whiz-bang experience of their lives. In fact, use of the word "whiz-bang" automatically discredits it from any consideration in their Top 10 life experiences.

Once I finally settled down as a teacher, a more vicious stress hit: infertility. I spent entire nights in paralytic worry. Will I ever have children? Will Josh and I grow old in a quiet home, just the two of us? We were blessed in 2009, when that problem resolved with the birth of our triplets. And, of course, as all parents know, there is nothing more relaxing than a newborn, right? Let me tell ya, try three at once. You'll be so relaxed, you won't know what to do with yourself! My nighttime worries had only begun. Despite the exhausting work of caring for three babies, I often found myself unable to sleep when my head hit the pillow.

I tried all sorts of higgery-jiggery to induce sleep: counting backwards from 500, drinking warm milk, limiting screen time. One mental exercise, though, sticks out in my mind: imagining myself in my ideal environment.

Oddly, despite my efforts to place myself in various exotic locales, my mind always conjured the exact same image:

A woman standing in an open prairie, leaning on a fence. She rests her head on her arms, folded loosely across the top fence-rail, and props one leg carelessly along the bottom. Her long hair is pulled back in a low ponytail, a few wisps escaping around her face. She gazes off into the distance, toward the faint outline of a mountain range. Far behind her stands a house, alone in the vastness. She turns to me and smiles, then stares back in her original direction.

I became obsessed with her.

Who was she? Why was she so calm? I wanted to be her. Would I have to move to Montana? Stop wearing make-up? Learn how to saddle up some dogies? (Learn what "saddle up some dogies" means?) She became my own little Mona Lisa. What was that smile about? Was she taunting me? Inviting me? What did she know that I didn't?

As I adopted minimalism, something about this woman became clear: my fixation with the image wasn't about her, it was about the space. She was not the most important part of the picture. The vast emptiness around her was.

I realized something else, too. As I slowly shed the burden of my stuff, I became more like her. I did not need to move to Montana or to an island in the middle of nowhere. I could create a more peaceful environment in suburban Ohio simply by creating more space in my home.

I have said many times, to people who've inquired about my minimalist habits, that the reason I do it is because it makes me feel calm. I no longer look about my house anxiously, fearing that my stuff will swallow me whole. I feel at peace. No vacation required.

I believe everyone feels this way when they encounter clutter-free space.

Take my classroom, for example. As I slowly began practicing minimalism at home, I did the same at work. I remember one day I donated a large red rolling cupboard to a new teacher. When my students came into my room and saw the bare corner, they were astounded. "What did you do?" they asked. "It feels different in here."

Some didn't say anything, though, and simply walked over to the space, raised their arms and twirled slowly in a circle. Let me remind you, these were 12 and 13-year-olds. Arms-up twirling isn't exactly a typical stance. Yet, confronted with the unexpected joy of open space, they could not help but adopt the universal body language of wonder and happiness.

There is something in all of us that attracts us to open spaces. I bet if you asked 100 people to imagine their ideal environment, 99 of them would name something that involved space: a beach, the woods, a field, a river, etc. I doubt anyone would describe their ideal environment as a crowded shopping mall, the bleachers at a soccer tournament, or a living room stuffed with toys and old magazines.

Yet, we consistently place ourselves in these environments every single day. It's no wonder we long for vacations! Vacation is not just a break from our daily routines; it is often a break from the overwhelming stress of our stuff.

So, here is my challenge for you: imagine yourself in your ideal environment. Got an image? Good. Now, create it. In your daily life. At work. In your house. In your garage. With your family. It is possible.

And in case you're wondering, I tend to sleep better lately. And the image of the woman on the prairie no longer mystifies me. Nowadays, when she turns to me with that secret smile, I know exactly what she's smiling about.

Think About It:

Imagine yourself in your ideal environment. Use all five of your senses. What do you see? Hear? Smell? Touch? Taste? Jot down ideas and details to remind yourself of this place.

CHAPTER 2

The Real Benefit of Owning Less

Minimalism has many benefits, ranging from more pleasing aesthetics to mental clarity, but when people ask me why I continue to strive toward this lifestyle, my answer is always the same: it just makes my life easier.

My House is Always Clean

A few months into my minimalism journey, my mother-in-law was due for a weeklong visit. Normally, the prospect of overnight guests sent me into an anxiety-fueled cleaning frenzy, due entirely to the state of my house, not my mother-in-law, who is a truly wonderful person.

My pre-guest routine involved much nervous surveying of my cluttered house, biting at my fingernails, and intense nagging at my husband and kids. But on this particular occasion, I looked around my newly minimized home in wonder, as a surprising truth slowly dawned on me ... my house was already clean.

It's been five years since that moment, and it's still true. My house is always clean.

I don't say this to brag, but to simply relate one of the unexpected benefits of becoming a minimalist: I have less stuff to clean; thus, my house is cleaner.

But don't get the wrong idea. If you stopped by on a Saturday morning, there would be toys on the floor and my kids would likely be constructing a fort out of cardboard and markers. My house is still a kid-friendly place, but it also happens to be relatively clean. At least, cleaner than it used to be.

Before embracing minimalism, when I packed my home with as much stuff as I could muster, much of my "cleaning" involved transferring piles of stuff from one undesirable location to another. *The stack of unopened mail? Hmm ... put it on the kitchen counter instead of the coffee table. The kids' toys? Shove them all in that ottoman instead of the corner.*

I thought people with consistently clean homes were anomalies. How did they do that, exactly? Sure, maybe some of them loved to clean, but maybe, just maybe, they had less stuff, making their houses less cluttered, making them, well, cleaner.

Think about it ... How easy is it to vacuum an uncluttered floor or wipe an empty countertop? Many of us perceive "cleaning" as difficult because we are actually performing two steps: 1) decluttering, followed by 2) cleaning. And of the two, let me tell you with authority: decluttering takes much, much longer.

I do my real cleaning (scrubbing floors, sinks, toilets, and the like) in small bits and pieces throughout the week, as necessary. It's never a big job. It rarely takes more than a few minutes. And the best part is, it's easy because *I don't have to declutter first in order to do it.*

If cleanliness isn't enough of a benefit for you to try minimalism, think of the time you will save. Your stuff absorbs your time. When my kids were toddlers, I spent around 10 minutes picking up toys every time I put them down for naps or nighttime. This equaled 20 minutes per day, which doesn't sound like much. But, 20 minutes per day is 2.3 hours per week or 120 hours per year, which is the equivalent of five full 24-hour days.

So basically, I spent five days each year just picking up *toys*. I don't know about you, but that is not how I want to spend my precious time here on Earth.

Once we owned less toys, my kids could put them away themselves. (Yes, even as toddlers.) Today, I still spend a few minutes tidying up every day, but it's nothing compared to what I used to do. Now, once my kids are in bed, I have nearly my entire evening to myself, to do things I really care about.

What do you want to do with your time? I'm guessing clean your house is not at the top of your list. At the risk of sounding like a cheesy motivational speaker: *Minimize your stuff to maximize your life.*

When you stop letting your stuff control your time and energy, you will find that you have energy left to do the things you really want to do, like read a book or call a friend or catch up on your favorite television series.

Or, if you're feeling like a real minimalist, to do absolutely nothing at all.

I Know What I Have

"I didn't even know I had this!" This is a phrase I regularly hear from clients. Said in a surprised voice often leaning toward bewilderment, this sentence exemplifies what happens when we own lots of stuff: our brains just can't keep track of it all. We end up storing the excess in bins and boxes to be "discovered" later.

This used to happen to me, too, but now I mostly know what I have everywhere in my house. (Note: this does NOT apply to the bins of mystery stuff Josh keeps in the attic. My avoidance of those bins reflects my strong commitment to marital harmony … and my lack of desire to get into an argument about whether or not Star Wars toys and 1980s baseball cards are legitimate tools for financing our kids' college educations.)

Knowing what I have means I know where to find things. For example, I used to keep multiple pairs of nail clippers all over my house. I'm not sure why I felt the need to be prepared for simultaneous hangnail emergencies in my bedroom, bathroom, and kitchen, but I kept them all "just in case." Now I own one pair of nail clippers per bathroom. (Yes, I am one wild rebel, folks.)

Silly as it may sound, having one pair of nail clippers makes my life easier because everyone knows where they belong. And if they aren't there, we can track down the last user and make him/her responsible for putting them back. This is much easier than searching for clippers all over the house, and it also teaches everyone to put things in their "home," as opposed to just dropping items wherever seems convenient.

I Know What I *Don't* Have

This is the flip side of knowing what you have, but just as important. It is helpful to know what you *don't* have, so that you don't waste time looking for it.

For example, I recently went to the attic in search of something I'd written during graduate school. It was a collaborative book, each student in my class had contributed a page, and it had an image on the cover that I wanted to accentuate a funny story I was telling a friend. I knew the only place the book could be was in my memorabilia tub, so I opened the tub, spent a minute rifling through, and realized it wasn't there. I must have decluttered it at some point.

I'll admit, I felt a twinge of disappointment that I wouldn't have the image for my story, but more than that, I *felt glad that I didn't spend another hour tearing my attic apart looking for it. I knew what I didn't have.* I was also comforted by the thought that I had kept in touch with several members of the class—who might not be minimalists!—and might have kept a copy of the book. I knew I could track down that picture, if necessary.

Knowing what you don't have is very comforting. It allows you to quickly move from panic mode: *Where is that serving dish from Grandma? I know it's here somewhere!*—to action mode—*Perhaps I can borrow a serving dish from a friend.*

There is very little in this life that cannot be borrowed, rented, or purchased again. Being a minimalist frees you from the perceived need to stockpile items, because you can more quickly investigate other resources (friends, neighbors, Craigslist) for obtaining things you need. This not only saves time, but a significant amount of stress.

Speaking of time, a study published in The Daily Mail found that people spend an average of 10 minutes per day looking for lost items. This equates to about 3,680 hours—or 153 days—over the course of a lifetime. I don't know about you, but I don't want to spend nearly half a year of my life searching for lost keys or wallets or nail clippers or silly things I wrote in college.

In other words, being a minimalist is the next best thing to going all *Back to the Future* and inventing your own flux capacitor. Okay, maybe that's a stretch. Sadly, being a minimalist has not resulted in a sweet 1980s DeLorean—or better yet, a dreamy 1980s Michael J. Fox—showing up in my driveway. Sigh.

But I do know that when I minimized my stuff, I maximized my time. Because my house is decluttered—thus, it always looks clean—I no longer nickel and dime my time away picking up toys, shoes, and the like. Because I know what I have and what I don't, I don't waste my time searching for things.

Yes, my life is still busy with three kids, a business, and the other commitments of just living, but I feel a much greater sense of freedom in my days now, because I no longer feel bound to my stuff. It doesn't control my time; thus, it doesn't control me.

It surprises me how often I hear people say, "I'm just so overwhelmed by my stuff." If you've ever said—or felt—this, I encourage you to imagine a life with less, a life where your possessions are not in control, you are. After all, we only get one shot at this life. Who do you want to be in charge of it? You or your stuff?

Think About It:

Approximately how much time do you spend each day decluttering and/or cleaning your house?

*How much time do you **want** to spend?*

*What is **one** area/aspect of your home (clothing, toys, tools, kitchen, etc.) that bothers you because it feels cluttered or overwhelming?*

*How would decluttering this **one** area make your life easier?*

CHAPTER 3

Thoughts on Trash & Treasure

I was taught the value of saving things at a very young age. Raised by a thrifty mom who was raised by a thrifty mom who survived the Great Depression, I learned the value of stretching my dollars and re-purposing items whenever possible.

Who needs fancy Tupperware when an old cottage cheese container will do? I'll admit, I still rinse out and re-use Ziploc bags whenever possible. And, while I try to tell myself I'm doing this to help the environment, it's actually because I can imagine my Grandma Cimini shaking her head at me if I didn't.

But, in a culture where many of us are not living hand-to-mouth, the urge to save items, especially if those items were "a deal," can result in a dangerous level of overconsumption. As a child in the 1930s, my grandmother had no risk of living in excess. There was no 24-hour big box store down the road where she could buy a cartload of cheaply-made plastic clearance items at her convenience. The saving habits she learned as a girl were logical for her time and helped her and her family survive.

However, we do ourselves a disservice in modern society if we attempt to save items as our grandparents did. Why? Because most of us have greater access to many, many more goods.

Don't get me wrong. I am not endorsing a "throw away" or "use it once and toss it" attitude. Quite the contrary. I think a commitment to purchasing, and using, a lesser amount of higher quality items provides untold benefits not only to our environment, but also to our world's neediest citizens and our own pocketbooks.

One Man's Trash

Owning less means throwing away less. Thus, minimalism is a strong commitment to keeping waste out of our landfills, an incredible gift to future generations. Re-using and recycling are wonderful habits; however, I often tell my clients: *it all becomes trash someday.*

Let me give you a scenario. Imagine I purchase a plastic water bottle and when I'm done drinking, I toss that bottle into the recycling bin. The bottle then becomes a fleece jacket, and that jacket is worn by someone for a year or two. When the person outgrows the jacket, he donates it to a thrift shop and it is eventually worn by someone else, who then donates it as well, and it is worn by three more people. Wow! I have done something good by recycling my water bottle, right?

Yes and no. I've kept that plastic out of the landfill for several years, which is admirable. But unless the base material (in this case, plastic) is compostable (in this case, no), it doesn't matter how many times it is recycled or how many people re-use it.

Eventually, that water bottle (now a fleece jacket) becomes landfill waste because plastic cannot be composted. How much better if I had purchased one high-quality reusable water bottle and used it for years, than to have repeatedly purchased cheap plastic bottles and recycled them, thus putting strain on the environment?

Now, take a moment and extrapolate the above scenario to dishes, clothing, tools, toys, furniture, media, books, interior décor, everything in our homes. Yikes.

Before we all start panicking, imagining mountain-high piles of landfill waste, let's take a reality check. *Humans are consumers. We must consume.* It is how we survive. And in today's world, we are blessed that we can recycle or re-purpose many of the items we need for survival. But let me suggest that we do Mother Earth a solid and give her one better: let's cut overconsumption off at the source by simply owning less.

If we own less, we have less that needs to recycled or repurposed. If we say a firm "No" to cheaply made goods, we don't even give those goods the chance to start putting a strain on our environment. If we purposely choose to buy just what we need—at the best quality we can afford—we will make incredible strides toward a better Earth for our grandchildren.

And that is something of which my own sweet grandma would most definitely approve.

Another Man's Treasure

Mahatma Gandhi once said, "Live simply so that others may simply live." As a man who epitomized a life lived in service to others, Gandhi would surely have approved of minimalism.

When you choose to own less, you are essentially saying that others—who are in great need—can have more. How so?

One of my main goals when working with a client is to help them let go of the items they no longer want or use. These items typically are in good shape and perfectly usable, which is why most of us hold on to them. *It's still good! How can I get rid of it?* But nearly all of these items can be donated to a variety of charities that will re-purpose them.

I used to volunteer at an overnight shelter for homeless women and children. Every night, each guest received a clean towel, sheets and basic toiletries. I was often in charge of distributing these items and I quickly realized how much of a difference basic supplies—a towel, a pillowcase—can make to those in a stressful situation.

Whenever I help clients declutter their linen closets, I always talk about this experience and clients usually end up donating a significant number of linens, which I happily drop off at the shelter.

When we live in excess it is easy to forget that others are barely getting by. When we deliberately and consciously choose to live with less, we are saying

"Yes, someone else can live with just what they need." I think this was what Gandhi meant by his quote.

Further, living with less frees us financially from the burdens of keeping-up-with-the-Joneses consumerism. Buying the latest gadgets, tools, and clothing will always put a hurt on our pocketbooks. When I adopted minimalism, I said a clear "No" to mindless shopping and "Yes" to shopping deliberately. I no longer cruise clearance aisles at stores, randomly picking up "deals" I didn't need in the first place.

When Josh and I first got married, I was unused to the heady combination of summers off—while Josh worked—and having true disposable income for the first time. I remember one of those early credit card bills from my first summer off from teaching.

"How did we spend an extra $1,000 this month?" I said, shocked as I looked at our high bill. There were no plane tickets or big-ticket purchases on the bill. However, as I scoured the charges line by line, I noticed a pattern: $30 here, $65 there. All on clothes I had found "on sale" at various stores. I was shocked by how much I had spent in little bits and pieces, never realizing what a bill I had racked up.

I'd love to say that I stopped random, purposeless shopping after that first bill, but I continued to practice this habit, although with slightly less excess, for years. When entering a store, I'd browse the clearance aisles, the dollar bins, the buy-one-get-one "deals" for items I did not need.

Let me tell you, there is no "deal" when you are buying something you don't need in the first place. I have spent thousands of dollars on "sale" items over the years, many of which I could have simply lived without.

And what could I have done with those thousands of dollars instead? Imagine if I had, instead of spending money here and there, donated it to causes I care about? What a difference my thousands of dollars would have made!

My credit card bill no longer contains spending surprises. I typically know what I spend and why. Don't get me wrong, I still need to go shopping. Unless you're planning to go all *Little House on the Prairie* and make your own soap and clothes, shopping is a necessity for most of us.

But I would urge you: shop with purpose. Know what you want before you head into the store. Ignore the clearance racks and seek out the items you truly love and need. Even if they aren't "on sale" I guarantee you will spend less in the end.

And, what can you do with that cushion in your pocketbook? Well, if you are so moved, you could make a charitable contribution to an organization of your choice. One of the best things I did when I adopted minimalism was consolidate my charitable giving to two main organizations. These were the organizations that sent me pamphlets with pictures of starving or sick children, the kind that made me feel guilty as I—typically—let those pamphlets sit in a pile of paper because I was too distracted and busy to write the check.

As I minimized my stuff and was better able to focus on my values, I contacted these two charities to set up monthly recurring donations, directly from my bank account. I can afford it. I'm no longer wasting my spare cash on cheap shoes and trinkets. I know that I'm making a very meaningful, purposeful contribution to two important causes every month. How much better than wasting that extra money on clearance t-shirts!

Cash Money, Baby

I'm supposing by now you've thought of yet another great advantage to minimalism ... a little more jingle in your pocket. I'm no mathematician, but I stand firmly behind this equation:

Buying less stuff = Having more money

And who wouldn't want a little more money to do with as they please? (As long as you don't spend it shopping for stuff you don't need, which by now you know is a major no-no!)

Because we don't worry about keeping up the Joneses or buying the latest this or that, Josh and I can afford to have regular date nights and take our kids on vacations. We also have cash on hand for emergencies, such as the air conditioning that just went out this morning and cost over $500 to fix (true story!). I didn't bat an eye as I wrote the check and I didn't put it on a credit card that I can't pay off.

Debt is a beast. Those of you living with credit card debt and creditors breathing down your neck already know this, but it bears repeating: debt is a burden and it will keep you from getting where you want to go in life.

If you want a serious plan to get out of debt, read Dave Ramsey's *Total Money Makeover*. If you want my two cents on the subject: stop buying crap you don't need.

What would you do if you were debt-free and had enough cash to cover your needs plus some saved for emergencies? Start a business? Switch careers? Take that vacation you've always dreamed of? Send your kids to college? Build an orphanage in Tibet?

Whatever your dream, realize that being a minimalist can help you get there, because although it sounds paradoxical—the less stuff you have, the more financial security you have.

So, cheers to a little more cash in your wallet! Who knew that all you had to do was let go of some stuff?

In Brief

Environmental devastation, worldwide poverty, and consumer debt culture are three staggeringly huge issues, and I do not attempt to suggest a solution within the confines of this book. (I'll address them all in my next book, *Rose Solves All the World's Problems in 200 Pages or Less*. It will cost about one million dollars per copy. Pre-order now.)

Yet, I would argue that the simple philosophy of minimalism—living with just what we need and love—can go a long way toward resolving the core issue at the heart of all three of these problems: overconsumption.

By choosing to live with less, we say "No" to mindless consumerism and "Yes" to allowing all of us to live a life where our basic needs are met and we have the financial freedom to pursue our dreams.

Think About It:

What would happen if you bought less things, but at the highest quality you could afford?

What excess items do you have in your home that would make a real difference to needy people in your community?

What types of philanthropic organizations excite you? What would happen if you consolidated your charitable giving to just 1-2 of these organizations?

How would your life be different if you did not live in debt?

CHAPTER 4

Cultivating a Minimalist Mindset

Being a minimalist is like being a rebel, but without all the tattoos and piercings. But hey, if they help you get in the minimalist spirit, feel free to get the tattoos and piercings!

I've found that the hardest part of minimalism is not sorting through items and deciding what to keep or let go. The hardest part is *thinking* like a minimalist. In fact, according to the New York Times, one market research firm study estimates that Americans are exposed to as many as 5,000 advertisements per day.

Advertisements are on our TVs, smart phones, even the sneakers our children wear to school.

Clearly, our culture is designed to make us want *more*. And it tells us to want more pretty much every single day. Wanting less is directly opposed to this agenda and it can feel awkward and strange. I'd like to share two mantras that might help you think like a minimalist: *remember the towels* and *remember the naked blue lady*. Clearly, I'm a fan of fun subheadings, but believe me, these do make sense!

Remember the Towels

One of the first projects I tackled on my minimalism journey was my linen cupboard.

It was a typical Saturday afternoon and I thought I'd spend a few moments getting this one small space in my home under control. As I opened the door and looked inside, though, I saw disaster—haphazardly piled towels, mismatched sheet sets, and tablecloths filled the space completely. I had two immediate urges:

1) Close the door and ignore this chaos.

2) "Organize" everything. Fold it neatly, put the towels all together, maybe get one of those space-saving bags to suck all the air out of the sheet sets so they fit better. Make it "look nice," which I knew, would not last for long.

I resisted these urges, but I list them here to let you know that they are normal. When faced with chaos, our immediate response is to ignore it. It's much easier to close the door than to deal with what's inside. It's also much easier to attempt to "organize" our items instead of minimize them. An entire industry of bins and baskets exists because of this urge!

So, I faced these urges and let them ride out. Then I emptied all the contents and sorted them into like-with-like piles: towels together, sheets together, etc. As I examined each pile, I asked myself the same question: "How many of these items do we *need*?"

This is a very different question from, "How can I organize this better?" If you look online, you will find a million ways to organize the items in your home. But if you have too much stuff, your attempts at simply organizing will fail. Your cute bins will overflow, the cupboard will get stuffed again, you will buy more and be unable to incorporate it into what you already have. Start your sorting from the perspective of *need*. It's a much more effective way to get your space under control.

Once I had my towels in a pile, I noticed that we had A LOT of them, way more than we could ever use in one laundry cycle. When we got married,

Josh and I registered for the number of towels recommended on our wedding registry. And it should come as no surprise that the folks who create wedding registries do not endorse minimalism!

So, I asked myself, "How many towels do we actually *need*?" The answer was simple: two for me, two for Josh, one for each of the kids, and two for guests.

But the idea of having just nine towels seemed crazy! The "what ifs" immediately popped into my brain:

- *What if there's a flood and I need towels to sop up water?*

- *What if a towel gets stained or dirty?*

- *What if I need to use a towel to soak up something gross, like blood or mud or an oil spill?*

I thought my minimizing had gone too far. *Only nine towels? I must be nuts!*

Again, I write these thoughts to let you know that they are normal. When faced with the prospect of minimizing our possessions, our inner squirrel often kicks in. It can feel "wrong" to let go of perfectly good items. (By now, though, you've hopefully realized it's not "wrong," just directly opposed to our society's consumer values. Remember, you're being a rebel!)

I was starting to sweat, so I brought Josh in for a consultation. To my utter surprise, when I suggested eliminating roughly half our towels, he seemed unfazed. "That sounds about right," he said. He may have just wanted to quickly escape the towel conversation to return to his man cave and watch sports, but either way, I had my answer.

So, we donated half our towels, all our excess sheets (we kept two sets per bed), and all our tablecloths. (Like most mothers of young children, I really have no need for a tablecloth ... like ever.) I donated everything to the homeless shelter I mentioned earlier.

And you know what? It's been over five years and not once has our towel cupboard been empty. I also have not purchased a single towel in that time.

This tells me two things:

1. I can live with a lot less than I think I can.

2. I can definitely live with a lot less than society tells me I *should*.

Being a minimalist starts with thinking like a minimalist. And a minimalist always thinks about what they *need*.

This is not the message you will find in advertising or on social media or across the street at the Joneses. Sadly, most messages in our culture are aimed at our wants. But I encourage you: *remember the towels*. When confronted with your possessions, simply ask yourself: how much do I *need*? This simple question will help you find the courage to free yourself from the excess.

Remember the Naked Blue Lady

My mom is an artist. She earned a degree in art education (a practical artist) and taught art in public schools for over 20 years. She used to paint and sculpt in her free time, which I think happened sometime before me and my three siblings were born. But I'm happy to report that she has returned to her artsy roots in her retirement.

She loves to give her art as gifts; thus, for her brother's wedding in 1974, she painted a large canvas of a naked blue lady for him and his wife. Now, let me explain. The lady is technically naked, but she is painted from the side and has her knees tucked up to her chin. No naughty parts visible. (A practical, modest artist.)

I had no idea of the existence of the naked blue lady until Josh and I rented our first apartment in Dayton in 2004. We visited my aunt and uncle, who asked how the new apartment was coming along.

"Great, but our walls are so bare," I said. "We can't afford nice paintings, so everything is kind of white-on-white right now."

My aunt's eyes lit up, as only the eyes of someone who's been holding on to her sister-in-law's painting of a naked blue lady for the past 30 years in the hopes of finding a proper owner can light up.

"I have just the thing!" Aunt Carol cried. She jumped up from her seat and dashed downstairs to the basement.

Ten minutes later, she emerged with a large, dusty canvas and a cloth.

"Your mom gave this to us for our wedding," she said, vigorously dusting the fame. "It will be just perfect for your apartment!"

Josh and I looked at the painting. We liked it. And not just because my mom painted it. We genuinely liked this tall lady, sitting in her relaxed pose, long hair flowing down her back.

"We'll take it," we said, although I don't think there really was another option in my Aunt Carol's mind.

My Uncle Mike, of course, couldn't resist spending a few minutes gently chiding his wife about her obvious regifting.

"Carol, I like that painting. Why don't we display it here? There's space above the mantle."

"Mike, we just don't need this naked lady. Rose and Josh need it."

"She's not naked," Uncle Mike said. "I see no nakedness."

"Mike. They want the painting. Give them the painting."

Oh, how I love family dynamics.

The best part of this story is that Josh and I now have a lovely naked blue lady who watches over our dining room table while our family eats, does homework, and checks email. We can't imagine our home without her.

So how does this relate to minimalism?

Minimalism does not mean having just the bare bones necessary for survival. It also means leaving space for the things you love, the things you value, the things that bring you great joy.

In other words, minimalism leaves plenty of room for the naked blue ladies of the world.

One of my favorite quotes is from poet and designer William Morris: "Have nothing in your house that you do not know to be useful, or believe to be beautiful."

Those two key words—*useful* and *beautiful*—are the checkpoints I use to decide if items are welcome in my home. Do I know it to be useful? Meaning, do I know this because *I actually use it*? Beware the pitfall of "potentially useful." Many of us have plenty of potentially useful items lying around, completely unused.

Also, do I believe it to be beautiful? If I consider something beautiful, I want to see and enjoy it every day. Thus, for me to keep something in my home, it must be either useful or beautiful or both.

In Brief

Minimalism focuses on what you need, like two towels per person, and what you love, like the naked blue lady. And who wouldn't want to live in a home surrounded only by the things they need and love? Your home is your castle; it's where you relax, make memories, and recharge to face the world outside. By designating your home as a sanctuary for only what you need and love, minimalism can help you transform your house into an oasis. After all, life is too short to not love where you live.

Think About It:

Which areas of your home make you want to just shut the door and ignore the chaos?

What would happen if you opened those doors and asked yourself which of the contents you actually <u>need</u>?

Which items in your home do you find beautiful? Do you have the space to enjoy these things? If not, what is keeping you from enjoying them?

What would happen if you only allowed useful and beautiful things inside your home?

CHAPTER 5

It's Just Stuff

My Grandma Dorothy is an amazing woman. Among her many accomplishments: giving birth to eight children in just over a decade, driving her own car until age 90, and making the best darn cheesy potatoes known to man.

Recently, at age 92, this grandmother of 21 and great-grandmother of 23 surprised the entire family when she calmly announced that she wanted to sell her house, where she still lived independently, and move to a senior living community. By the way, her biggest complaint about the senior community— which she refers to as "The Funny Farm"—is that it's full of old people.

If you haven't figured it out yet, my grandma is more with-it than most of us, whether we live on The Funny Farm or not.

After her move, I approached her for some advice. I had been asked to give a downsizing presentation at a local senior living community and I needed ideas. So, I cornered Grandma during Thanksgiving dinner and asked her what she'd say to those considering the move to senior living. She thought for moment, then gave a very succinct, Grandma Dorothy-like response.

"Two things," she said. "First, I wish I had started downsizing sooner, and second, it's just stuff!"

She punctuated this second piece of advice with a classic Grandma Dorothy gesture, flipping both hands away from herself, accompanied by a quick frown and audible, "Uh!" I have seen her make this gesture when discussing everything from the number of tattoos on young people these days ("Even the young girls!") to a meal she considered overindulgent ("The salads. You've never seen so many different kinds of salads in your life!"). It's one of her signature moves, a washing of the hands, a way of saying, "Let the rest of them enjoy themselves, but I'll have none of that, thank you."

Her advice—*It's just stuff*—combined with this gesture have stuck with me ever since.

No matter how old we are or what stage of life we're in, whether we're contemplating a child's tea set or a set of mixing bowls or a garage full of power tools, *it's just stuff.*

Whether we're worried about what to do with all our old technology or how to contain our kids' toys or how to preserve all those memorabilia T-shirts from college, *it's just stuff.*

Whether we're worried if our children will someday want our dishes or furniture or artwork, *it's just stuff.*

I think Grandma Dorothy's message is: *it's not worth worrying about all the things you own.* Because if you do, you let them own you. Fretting about what will happen to your baseball cards or your dining set detracts from the quality of life you're living now.

I'm not just referring to elderly people. I've met plenty of younger folks who worry incessantly about their things. *What to do with all these Legos my kids have? Ugh ... my closet is an overwhelming disaster! I hate my basement ... it's still full of boxes from when we moved in.*

I think my grandma, in the twilight of her life, realizes something the rest of us would do well to remember: *you can't take it with you.* All the stuff, all the things, all the collections will be left when we're gone, and what then? What good was all our fretting and organizing and worrying? How much better would it be to spend our precious, fleeting time on Earth holding hands with those we love, making pancakes from scratch, and laughing with friends over a glass of wine?

I think we'd all agree that yes, we want to live our lives like that, lives full of meaningful experience.

So whaddaya say, why not let the rest of them enjoy themselves and consciously say a firm, "No, thank you" to a life monopolized by consumer goods? Why not decide—right now—to live a more fulfilling life, a life with plenty of room for your values and loved ones?

Because, like my grandma says, whether you're 18 or 80, the time to downsize is *now*. And remember, it's just stuff.

Think About It:

Does your stuff get in the way of living the life you want? How so?

What kinds of things would you do if you didn't have to deal with your stuff so often?

What would happen if you took Grandma Dorothy's advice—it's just stuff—and applied it to just one area of your home?

CHAPTER 6

How To: The LESS Method™

My friend Jon designs space satellites. That's right, he's a for-real rocket scientist. I once got into a conversation with him about electrons, which I quickly exited when I realized two things: 1) Besides the occasional, "I see" or "I understand," (which, by the way, were complete lies) I could in no way contribute to the conversation, and 2) I really should have failed high school physics.

So, let me set you at ease. Minimizing is not rocket science.

Yet, most of us avoid it. Why? Because decluttering is overwhelming. Facing our stuff means facing our emotions, many of which we'd like to avoid. When we declutter, we often have to face uncomfortable emotions like:

- **Regret:** *Ugh ... why did I buy this? I spent so much money and I never use it.*

- **Guilt:** *Aunt Jean gave this to me. I can't let it go. What would she think?*

- **Fear:** *What if I need this someday?*

All these worries swirl together into one anxiety tornado and we often find it's easier to just shut the door.

But I urge you, open it. Let me tell you how.

Make the Time

I very intentionally titled this section "Make the Time" as opposed to its more popular cousin "Find the Time," because I think it's important to recognize the subtle—yet vital—difference between the two.

When we say that we can't do something because we can't "find the time" it's as if we believe there are hidden pockets of time in our life just waiting for discovery, as if some wily leprechaun has hidden a pot of time gold and all we have to do is locate it and—voila!—we'll be flush with the time needed to accomplish all the things we want to.

We all know that's not true.

Time is a concept created by humans. We made it. Thus, we cannot "find" time, but the good news is we can "make" it. And I encourage you to start making some right now.

I know, I know, this is the hardest part of accomplishing anything in life, right? We're all pressed for time. (By the way, if you're feeling a major time crunch, reread Chapter 3 on how minimizing can help you reclaim some of those sweet hours in your day.)

I know all about being pressed for time. Like right now. I'm writing a book and do you know all the other things I could be doing? Just think of all the email I could be checking and laundry I could be folding and cute cat videos I could be watching. Wow! All of those things would keep me really "busy" … avoiding the one thing I really want to get done: writing.

If decluttering your home is important to you, make it a priority and put it on your calendar. Hire a babysitter, turn off your phone, and commit yourself to doing something that matters to your peace of mind.

I'd love to think that the reason my clients are successful during our sessions is due to my sparkling personality, wit, and minimizing suave. But really, I know it's because—when they make an appointment with me—they are *making time* to change their lives. They are boldly declaring, "For the next three hours I shall do nothing else but deal with the chaos in this garage!" That's a strong statement, and one that will surely get some results.

I urge you, make time. Make an appointment with yourself to do this thing that you desperately want to do. Block it out on the calendar. Incentivize yourself with a treat—ice cream, an adult beverage, a Netflix marathon—if you keep the appointment. Invite a friend to help you. (Note: You'll definitely need to incentivize that friend with the aforementioned treats!) Do whatever it takes to make yourself keep this appointment, and I guarantee you, it will get done.

If you're wondering how much time you'll need, I recommend starting small. Most of my client sessions last 3-4 hours, but they have me by their side to keep them motivated. (Okay, so maybe my sparkling personality does matter, after all.)

Start with whatever amount of time you can scrape together, maybe just 30 minutes or an hour. Or if you're really crunched for time, visit LessTheBook. com and register for my *5 Minutes or Less Checklist,* a one-page list of minimizing tasks that you can do in—literally—under five minutes each! Just set a timer on your phone and do as much as you possibly can before it rings. Every minute brings you closer to your goal!

Planning to declutter your entire abode? Good for you! It is possible if you make the time and allow yourself some one-step-at-a-time grace. When I decluttered my entire house, it took about eight months. I'm not recommending that as a timeline for everyone. That's just how long it took me.

I didn't work on it every day. I had 3-year-old triplets and a full-time job outside the home—I was lucky if I remembered to brush my teeth every day! But I worked steadily, here and there, on weekends and naptimes and strange minimizing adrenaline rushes that sometimes came upon me after my kids went to bed. Channel your inner tortoise and remember that slow and steady wins the decluttering race.

I'd like to share one of my favorite personal mantras with you: *you always have enough time to do exactly what you want to do.* If you really want to run a marathon, you'll make the time to train. If you really want to eat healthier, you'll make the time to meal plan. And if you really want to minimize your stuff, you'll make the time to address each closet, drawer, and cubby, one small step at a time. And it will get done.

But I urge you, above all, don't worry about how much time you may or may not have, and *just start.*

Here's how.

Supplies

Like any project, you'll first need to gather some supplies, which you probably already have. (Again, not rocket science.) Here are the basics you need to tackle any decluttering project:

- Black trash bags

- White trash bags

- Empty cardboard boxes

- Black permanent marker

- Painter's tape

- Blank paper

I bet you could get up off your couch right now and gather these supplies in about 10 minutes. And while you're at it, have a snack. You're going to need some energy for all the minimizing you're about to do!

The LESS Method™

If you're going to successfully tackle your clutter, it helps to have a systematic approach. We often feel a very high level of anxiety when facing an overwhelming space. I see this in my clients' faces and body language when they open the doors to their stuffed closets and basements. They grimace, sigh, bite their lips, and cross their arms protectively. Some even cry.

That might sound extreme, but these are very normal responses to the emotional stress caused by clutter. Remember Chapter 1: humans naturally desire open spaces, so it makes sense that those cluttered corners raise our cortisol levels!

The LESS Method™ will give you a starting point, a plan, a way to move past the overwhelm and get cracking. It will also help you maintain your space once it is minimized. It stands for:

Lay Out Your Vision & Purpose

Empty

Sort It Twice

Systemize

Alright! Now you should be all set to declutter like a boss! What? You want more details about each of these awesome steps? Oh, do read on ...

Step 1: Lay Out Your Vision & Purpose

When facing a cluttered space, it's tempting to jump right in and begin sorting. Resist this urge. It's kind of like getting so excited about a road trip that you hop into your car and start driving without a map. If you did that, you would probably end up lost. Similarly, if you jump right into your clutter, you will end up overwhelmed and probably quit.

Before you put a single item in a donation box or trash bag, *take a moment to step back and reflect on how you want this space to look and function.* Laying out your vision and purpose is like getting the lay of the land, establishing a point of reference for where you are and where you want to go. It gives you a basic roadmap that helps you know if you're headed in the right direction. And whether you're taking a road trip or clearing clutter, this is critical if you want to get where you're going.

To start thinking about VISION, ask yourself questions like this:

- If I walked into this room and it looked perfect, what would it look like?

- If I could wave a magic wand and transform this space, what would I see?

- What are my goals for this space?

Having a strong vision is important, because humans do our best work when we start from vision. Some people call this beginning with the end in mind. You've probably seen Olympic athletes just moments before competition, eyes closed, envisioning themselves completing the perfect long jump, landing the triple twist, or entering the water with nary a splash. These visions—essentially glimpses of their future success—help them perform better.

Vision gives us confidence, lets us know what we're working toward, and helps us stay focused during the myriad distractions that can—and probably will—crop up on our way to getting there.

Take your black marker and write "VISION" on a piece of blank paper. Then close your eyes and imagine how you want this space to look. Go as crazy as you want. It's your imagination! Now open your eyes and write down what you imagined. Use painter's tape to attach this paper to the wall.

Here's an example of a typical **VISION** statement for a garage:

- Lots of floor space to park cars

- Everything easy to find, with labels

- Shelves for all the tools

- Bigger stuff hanging on the walls

- Open space to do woodworking

After you have a solid vision, start thinking about **PURPOSE**. Again, ask yourself questions to help you think through the reason this space exists in your home:

- What is the purpose of this space?

- How do I want it to function?

- What do I need this space to do for me?

- What types of activities do I do in here?

- Who else uses this space?

Get as specific as you can when answering these questions, avoiding general statements like "to store stuff." Having a fuzzy purpose makes it difficult for both you and those you live with to know what belongs where. This can quickly result in a room cluttered with random things, which is not the goal of minimizing!

In a garage, a **PURPOSE** statement might include:

- Sporting equipment

- Lawn care and gardening supplies

- Woodworking

- Tools

- Holiday decorations

- Car care supplies

- Park cars

Think of every possible thing you want this space to do for you and write it down, then tape your **PURPOSE** paper next to your **VISION** on the wall.

Why go to all this trouble? Because, *once you know your vision and purpose, you've won half the battle.* You've made your map and now you know where you want to go. In other words, you've already decided what stuff will stay and what needs to be shown the door.

For instance, in the garage example, if you came across a tub of college memorabilia and weren't sure what to do with it, you could look back at your purpose list—memorabilia is not listed, thus it should probably be located elsewhere.

Of course, if you decide that the garage is the best place to store your memorabilia, you can amend the sign. It's just paper and markers, not the Ten Commandments. The goal is to start storing your possessions *intentionally*, not just dumping them wherever there's space. This is how you start thinking like an organized person.

Knowing a space's vision and purpose gives you a roadmap, something to refer to when you feel lost in your clutter. This might seem like a step you could skip, but I urge you not to. In fact, I have occasionally skipped this step with clients, always to my deep regret, because I then see how much harder our session is.

Step 2: Empty

I've never broken up a rowdy fraternity party, but after cleaning out many closets and basements, I think I'd be well-suited to the task. If you want to restore order to a chaotic scene, do what officers do immediately upon arrival: *Everybody out!* When it comes to your stuff, this means *completely empty the space.* Yes, I said completely. Every stray sock, every unopened box from your last move, every last little crumpled receipt from the back of the drawer needs to come out into the light of day.

Again, this is another tempting step to skip. I hear you asking, "Wouldn't it just be easier take out the things I don't want and leave the rest?"

Nope. And here's why:

When things have lived in a certain place for a long time we start to no longer see them. Our eyes get so used to seeing the collection of owl figurines on top of the bookshelf that we no longer notice them.

Humans are attracted to the new, the novel, the different. We notice what is unfamiliar. Thus, if clutter is our "normal" we will not be very discerning unless we shake up the order of things. And the best way to do that is to remove every single item and appraise it.

Removing every item allows you to see your space in a new light, as if you are moving in for the first time. Remember the excitement of moving into your home? You saw the empty closets and rooms and envisioned possibilities. You started imagining where your favorite chair would go, your collection of glass paperweights.

You were excited about how you would arrange the space. Emptying the space completely allows you to re-see it in just this way, with fresh eyes. This will allow you to make better use of your space, rearranging it to better suit your life.

But what if the space is large, like an entire basement?

I often deal with large spaces—entire garages, basements, or large living areas. It would be difficult to completely empty these types of spaces. However, you can simply "chunk" the space into smaller parts. For example, you could address just one corner or bookshelf or 2x2 foot space. If you're not sure where to start, I recommend beginning at the doorway and moving top-to-bottom, left-to-right, clockwise around the room.

As you empty the shelves and drawers, put everything on the floor, if possible. If the floor is too cluttered to do this, move items to a different room. (Again, this is why starting near the door is helpful!) You may not have enough room to set things on the floor or even in another room. In that case, use a folding table or large box as "floor space" for the time being.

You will need to move slowly, tableful and boxful at a time, but you will make progress. And quickly you will see some sweet floor space emerge! Awesome! More room to sort!

One last tip: as you empty the space, toss obvious trash: crumpled receipts, packaging, clothing tags, broken or very dirty things. This will save you the hassle of dealing with it later.

Step 3: Sort It Twice

Don't hate me, but you have to sort your items twice. Here's why:

One of my favorite clients is a bubbly mom of three young children. She's a hugger, a vibrant spirit, the kind of mom who laughs easily and gets on the floor to play with her kids. She also struggles with clutter.

She hired me to organize her 5-year-old son's bedroom. The initial scene was a little slice of chaos—toys, clothing, and games were scattered all over the room. As we started working, I noticed my client becoming more and more distracted.

She picked up a small piece of black plastic.

"I know what this goes with … " she said, chewing her lip and looking around. "It goes with … the train track! It's part of the Christmas train he got from his grandma!" She lifted the piece in victory and began walking across the room to put it away. About halfway there, she noticed a stray soccer cleat sticking out from under a stuffed elephant.

"Augh! I've been looking for this! I just told him the other day that he needed to find this cleat! I'm going to put it in his bag right now."

She left the room with the soccer cleat, plastic train piece still in hand.

A few minutes later she came back and noticed an action figure with a broken arm. She picked this up and carried it to the kitchen to fix it.

This back-and-forth continued for about 10 minutes before I gently said, "You know what? Why don't you go play with your kiddos and I'll get all of this sorted into piles? Then you can come in and make decisions."

"Are you sure? Shouldn't I be in here with you?"

"If you want, but I'm not going to throw anything away without you here. And it'll be easier for you to make decisions once everything is in piles with similar things."

The relief that flooded her face was priceless. She went off to play with her kids, and I spent the next hour emptying her son's room into like-with-like piles on the floor.

When she returned, she sat comfortably on the bed while I brought piles to her for decisions: keep, donate, or trash. In just over an hour, the job was done.

This example illustrates the importance of sorting twice: first into piles of like-with-like and then into piles of what you will keep. Let me explain a bit more about these two sorting steps.

1st Sort: Like-with-Like

As you can tell from the above story, my client was pretty distracted at the beginning of our session. That's because she could not see the categories of stuff within her son's room. It would be like walking into a grocery store without designated aisles. Food would just be randomly scattered throughout the store. You'd have no idea where the oranges or milk or bread were located, so you'd wander aimlessly, searching for the items you needed, finding things you didn't expect, and forgetting what you were looking for in the first place.

Shopping like this would use up a lot of energy and you probably wouldn't have much in your cart to show for it, besides a bunch of bruised bananas and a box of toxic-looking Pop-Tarts. And while my kids would consider that a fine meal, I think most of us would leave a store like that full of nothing but frustration.

Many of us try to organize our homes this way, wandering aimlessly from pile to pile, losing ourselves and our mission in the process. And this is why many of us give up.

So, I encourage you: make sorting easier on yourself and put all your items into like piles first. Sorting into like-with-like makes it obvious how much you have. Often, clients are surprised to discover they own 37 screwdrivers or 52 coffee cups. Grouping makes it easier to let go of excess items because you may, for the first time, realize exactly how much you have.

Here's a typical list of piles I might make in a little boy's room:

- Stuffed animals
- Cars
- Trains
- Games
- Books
- Crafts

- Clothing

- Decor

- Randoms

- Memorabilia

A Word on Randoms and Memorabilia

Your like-with-like piles will be different, of course, depending on your space and your personality. However, no matter what space you are sorting, I strongly encourage you to make piles for the last two categories on the list: randoms and memorabilia.

I always find random items that aren't part of an obvious group: a telescope, a rubber bouncy ball, a plastic bracelet a child won at school, a keychain. These items don't belong to a larger group, so I put them all together.

Also, no matter what room you are in, you will find memorabilia. Believe me, I've even found memorabilia in people's bathrooms! Memorabilia is any item you are saving not to use or to display, but to remind you of something. Often, we think of memorabilia as just postcards and pictures, but it can span a large variety of items. For years, in fact, my dad kept the car he used to pick my mom up for their first date. Talk about some heavy memorabilia!

I often find memorabilia in bedroom closets, where people tend to store collections of T-shirts from activities they used to participate in. My clients usually aren't planning to wear these shirts again; they're purely for memory. Thus, they don't belong in the closet.

For now, separate all your memorabilia into a box (or boxes, let's be real!), label it, and put it somewhere else—your attic, your basement, it really doesn't matter. As long as it's all together, you're good. You will address it eventually, but at this early stage in the process, if you stop to wander down memory lane, or worse, try to make the hard decision of what memorabilia to keep and toss, you will seriously halt your minimizing progress.

Just get it all together and get it out of your current space. I'll explain how to deal with it in Chapter 12.

2nd Sort: Decide

Once you have like-with-like piles, it's decision time! This step should be relatively easy, now that you know exactly how much you have. Take a moment to look back at your VISION and PURPOSE signs. They're posted on the wall, right? Remind yourself what *belongs* in this space. Because you have a clear vision and purpose, you've already decided what stays and goes. Now you just need to get things where they belong.

Start with an easy pile, one that has a lot of items. Typically, the more items in a pile, the easier it is to let go of some of them. For example, in a child's room, I often start with stuffed animals.

Word of Caution: DON'T start with Randoms or Memorabilia. Remember, memorabilia will be exiting this space to be dealt with later. And I always sort Randoms last, after the more obvious piles have been dealt with.

Pick up each item, and *go with your gut.* Yes or No? Is this something you want to keep? Is it useful and/or beautiful? Does it suit your vision and purpose?

Make decisions as quickly as possible, relying strongly on that first gut instinct. Often, I can tell what decision clients will make based on their body language when they pick items up. If they sigh, grimace, or let out an audible, "Ugh ... " I know that item is destined for the donation bag.

If you have difficulty going with your initial feeling, here are some basic questions to help you decide whether or not you should keep something:

- Is this my favorite? (In other words, in a group of similar items, would I choose this one?)

- How does this item make me feel?

- If I lost it, would I replace it?

- Would I take it with me if I moved?

- Would I buy it again?

- If I needed this is the future, how much would it cost to replace it? (If the answer is less than $20, I recommend you let it go. The chance of you ever needing it is slim, and if you do, $20 is not going to break your bank.)

- What's the worst thing that would happen if I let go of this?

As you decide, sort your items into basic piles:

- Keep

- Donate

- Trash

- Elsewhere

- Sell

Keep

These are the items that fit with your vision and purpose, the ones that will eventually be returned to the space when you are finished. These are your treasures, your go-to's, the items that help you live your life and bring you joy. They are beautiful, useful, or both. For now, keep your keepers right there on the floor. We'll put them away later.

Donate

These are items that you no longer need, but could be useful to others. Put your donations into white trash bags (to differentiate them from actual trash) or boxes (for awkward or delicate items, like toasters or dishes).

Remember the social benefits of minimalism we talked about in Chapter 3 and donate with a happy heart! Also, I very strongly urge you to find one local charity that accepts a wide variety of donations and donate all your items there. Often, clients slow down the process when they try to donate to niche donation sites (shoes to Charity A, toys to Charity B, books to Charity C, and so on).

If your goal is to seriously minimize the excess in your home, you don't have time for that. Also, if you feel like you must parse your donations this way, I must ask: Is this a procrastination technique? In other words, are you intentionally slowing down the donation process to delay letting go of items?

Trash

I probably don't need to say much about this one. We all know what trash is. Use your black bags for trash so you don't confuse it with donations. As you bag your trash, keep in mind the words in Chapter 3: *it all becomes trash someday.*

Often, clients feel guilty about the amount of trash they generate during a session. This is normal. When you undertake a serious minimizing mission, you will generate more trash than usual for a short time. However, I can happily tell you that this drops off and you will create significantly less trash thereafter as a result of adopting a minimalist lifestyle.

Remember, *minimalism is probably the most environmentally friendly thing you can do.* From here on out, you will produce much less trash because you will check your consumption at the door and bring less into your home. But before you can do that, you have got to clear the plate. So, take a deep breath, fill those trash bags, and consider leaving a kind tip for your trash man. Spread the love.

Elsewhere

As you sort, you will find items that don't belong in this space, but belong somewhere else in your home. Set aside your Elsewhere items and return them to their proper homes at the end of the session. DON'T stop sorting to take Elsewhere items to their homes now! Doing that will cause you to lose focus on the task at hand. (Remember my client who left the room to return her son's soccer cleat? That could be you!) Make and tape an Elsewhere sign near the door to collect all these items.

You may want to make separate Elsewhere piles if you find you have many things that need to go to particular destinations. For example, it might be helpful to create a "To work" or "To sister-in-law" pile. But again, don't stop sorting to hop in your car and drive to work or your sis-in-law's right now!

Sell

Last but not least, you could create a sell pile. I say "could" because I strongly urge you not to. Why? Because selling takes your time, and honestly, it's often just not worth it. If you need more convincing of this, visit RoseLounsbury.com and read my blog post "Why Selling Stuff Is a Waste of Your Time."

Remember, your goal is to minimize the amount of stuff in your home. Spending hours posting and commenting on Buy/Sell/Trade groups doesn't help you accomplish that. Also, if you feel the need to sell lots of items, I must ask again: Is this procrastination? Are you collecting items to "sell" because you aren't ready to let them go?

Step 4: Systemize

Alright! Give yourself a high-five for some serious decluttering! By now your closets and drawers should be breathing quite a bit easier and you are ready for the final LESS Method™ step: Systemize.

This is where you will return your keepers in a way that makes logical sense. You'll focus on creating homes for all your precious items and labeling them, if necessary. You'll also start practicing some habits to maintain this space. Before you do that, though, take a moment to do three vital post-decluttering tasks:

1. Take out your trash

2. Put donations in your car (or call to arrange an ASAP charity pickup)

3. Relocate Elsewhere items to their proper homes

Obviously, you understand the importance of taking out the trash, but I find that people often neglect to do the other two tasks. This is a big mistake. *You must get unwanted items out of your space quickly.* There is nothing worse than working hard to declutter your home and then letting piles of donations or Elsewhere items hang out in your closet for months. If you do this, you've basically just relocated the clutter you worked so hard to remove.

True story: my friend's sister once decluttered her closet but left all the clothes she wanted to donate on a chair in her bedroom. A few months later, her sweet husband surprised her with a trip for their anniversary and, to make it a true surprise, he packed for her. Guess what he packed? Yep. All those clothes on the chair. After spending a week in ill-fitting, out-of-style clothing, she learned her lesson on why you should get donations to the car right away!

Grab a laundry basket and load it up with Elsewhere items, then go on a journey around your house, returning everything. Don't worry if you don't have the perfect home for these items. Often, clients don't want to return Elsewhere items because they feel like they are just adding more stuff to a different cluttered space in their homes. That's good! That means you know where you're headed next! I always say that minimizing one space puts pressure on another. It tells you the next stop on your journey. Important information!

Now you are alone in a freshly minimized space with just your most beautiful and useful items before you. Take a moment to enjoy this! How wonderful to have just your favorite things, exactly where they belong.

At this point, assign each item a "home" in this space. Sometimes people agonize over exactly where items should go, but it's really not that complicated. Again, go with your gut and just put your things where they make the most sense.

When I first started minimizing, I would patrol my countertops before I went to bed, picking up any stray items and asking aloud, "Where is your home?" Lucky for me, no one was around to witness this act of domestic crazy, and it helped me find logical homes for all those little things in my house.

If you find that a bin or basket would be helpful to corral items, now is the time to go buy one, or better yet, use one you already have! I bet you emptied plenty of them in Step 2. If you don't have a pretty bin or basket, don't worry.

Grab a shoebox, a plastic zipper bag, a 9x13 pan from your kitchen, whatever you can find to hold those items in place. You can go out and buy something pretty later on.

As you put things in their homes, consider whether or not you should label the home to make it obvious. My two favorite labeling supplies are really fancy: a black permanent marker and painter's tape. I create 90% of my client's labels this way. Painter's tape sticks to most surfaces and is easily removable with no damage to walls and counters.

Sure, it doesn't look like the pages of a magazine, but who lives in the pages of a magazine? What's most important is that you and everyone you live with know where things belong. If you want to invest in fancy labels later, great. Or, if you find that you don't need the labels anymore, you can peel them off, easy peasy.

I once labeled all the fronts of a client's kitchen cupboards with painter's tape to help her and her husband remember where things belonged. I told her to leave the tape up as long as she needed and peel it off once the system became second nature.

Maintenance

It would be so wonderful if your newly minimized space would stay looking like this forever, right? There are only two ways for that to happen:

1) Hermetically seal off the room and allow no one to enter, ever.

2) Practice a few simple habits to maintain it.

I opt for #2, but hey, if you have access to some large plastic sheeting and can afford to hire a security guard, feel free to try #1.

I recommend adopting two basic habits to help you maintain your new system. These habits play really well together and require very little time, so there is no reason not to give them a try!

Maintenance Habit #1: The Constant Donation Box

A constant donation box is just that: a box. That is constantly in your house. For donations. Mine is on my closet floor and it used to contain copy paper. Whenever we have something we want to donate, we just put it in the box. When the box is full (or let's be honest, when the box is overflowing and I have stuff piling up all around it), I fill up a few white kitchen trash bags and *immediately put them in my car* for donation drop off the next time I'm out.

I keep a roll of white kitchen bags in the box just for this purpose. Don't take the actual box to the donation site, because you might donate the box and then you are in danger of quitting the habit!

I always tell people that if they want to adopt just one habit to simplify their lives, start a constant donation box. You can have one in your house, or one on every floor, or one in every room if you are really serious! The reason the donation box is so powerful is because it makes donating a daily habit, as opposed to a special event.

I used to wait and wait until I couldn't stand the clutter for one more minute and do a tornado-like purge session throughout my entire house. This happened once a year or so. I call this "special event" minimizing and it's not very effective. It's hard and exhausting and results in much nagging at those sweet people you live with.

Now everyone in our house adds items regularly to the donation box, and it keeps the clutter at bay. I probably take a bag of donations to Goodwill once a month, which still surprises me, since I consider myself a minimalist. It's amazing how much stuff trickles into our lives, even when we are vigilant about keeping it out.

Maintenance Habit #2: The One In/One Out Rule

You've probably all heard this one, but I'm giving it its own subtitle anyway because it is SO IMPORTANT. The one in/one out rule basically says that when you get something new, you let something old go.

I used to think people who followed this rule were weird. I remember overhearing one of Josh's aunts talking about a shopping trip where she bought a new sweatshirt and her husband told her in the store that she had to donate an old one when she got home. *What kind of life is that?* I thought. *Craziness!*

And now look at me, just another loony in the bin.

The one in/one out rule is absolutely the most important habit you need to take on if you are going to maintain a minimalist home. It is the only way I have found to keep the clutter from creeping back, because believe me, it will try. You're going to get gifts for Christmas, you're going to need to buy a new printer, and your neighbor is going to drop off a bag of hand-me-down clothes for your kiddos. This is life. We are consumers and we must consume stuff to live. So, take charge of that stuff with a one in/one out policy.

I used to think this rule had to be apples-to-apples. For instance, if I bought new shoes, I thought I had to get rid of a pair of shoes. Now, though, I take a more liberal view. As long as I donate *something* when I get something new, I'm cool. So, if I get a new pair of shoes, but donate an old sweater or a set of oven mitts or a coffee cup, I'm still following the rule.

It's all about the habit of taking something in and letting something go. It doesn't really matter what that something is.

This is especially helpful with kids. (Yes, they follow this rule, too!) I used to make them donate a similar toy when they got a new toy, but I ran into a big, soft, fuzzy roadblock: stuffed animals. My kids love stuffed animals, and not in the just-at-bedtime way that most kids do.

Yes, they sleep with them, but stuffed animals are my kids' toy of choice. They play with them daily, create elaborate parties with the animals as guests of honor, and know each animal's individual birthday. In fact, each of my kids' top gift requests last Christmas were stuffed animals. (Stuffed sharks, to be exact. You should have seen Santa's face when my kids—in turn—asked specifically for a stuffed mako, blue, and whale shark. We nicknamed 2017 "Aquatic Christmas.")

In any case, when I tried to get my kids to let go of a stuffed animal when getting a new one, it was a no-go. I realized that forcing them to donate a stuffed animal might actually irreparably harm them, so instead, when faced with one in/one out, I just ask my kids to find any toy they could donate in exchange for their new one. They've gotten so used to this that they don't even question it. They just head to their bedrooms and find something to let go.

In Brief

The LESS Method™ is a practical, systematic way to minimize the excess in your home. You can use this method to clear your clutter, room by room, closet by closet, drawer by drawer. And once you've practiced it a few times, it will feel like second nature. I always love when I go to clients' homes for our third or fourth session and I see that they have ingrained this system and can start to take the minimizing lead.

To Summarize:

Lay Out Your Vision & Purpose: Decide how you want the space to look and function. Make vision and purpose signs and tape them to the wall.

Empty: Everything out! And I mean everything!

Sort It Twice: First into like-with-like; then into keep, donate, trash, elsewhere and sell.

Systemize: Give all your keepers a home and make it obvious, using containers and labels, if necessary. Practice using a constant donation box and following the one in/one out rule to keep the clutter from coming back!

CHAPTER 7

Start With Your Own Stuff

"I don't know where to start!" is a phrase I often hear from overwhelmed clients. If you have many areas of your home that need decluttering, it can feel impossible to know where to begin. I once felt this way, too. There was so much stuff in my house and only one of me. Where does one begin?

I only have one rule about getting started: *start with the areas under your jurisdiction.* In other words, deal with your own stuff before you try to deal with everyone else's stuff.

Establish Goodwill

Dealing with your own stuff establishes goodwill and respect among you and those wonderful people you live with. This is important, especially if you have kids. Parents (myself included) often complain that their kids are messy, and that the chaos in the home is due entirely to the children. Now, as a mother of triplets, I can attest to the fact that children and their accompanying stuff most definitely add an element of chaos to a home.

Anyone who has had a child understands this. I remember my friend Scott, after having his first child, told me, "I never understood why you were so into writing about having less stuff. It seemed like kind of a weird hobby. But now I totally get it."

I never felt the need to minimize before I had kids, which is normal. When we're living with just our stuff, it's much easier to deal with, even if we have excess. I think because the addition of children to a home often precedes the feeling of physical overwhelm, we tend to blame the kids for creating the chaos. When actually, we chose to bring those children into our home, and if we didn't clear enough space for them and their things—or we didn't take the time to teach them how to maintain and put away their own things—the fault is ours.

I'm not trying to heap parent guilt on you (we all have plenty of that already!) but to help you see that *children don't inherently bring clutter into homes*. Adults do. So, if our homes are cluttered and uncomfortable, it is not fair to blame our children for this.

Establishing goodwill extends to anyone else who might have joined your household, too, even adults. I once worked with a couple who had gotten married later in life, and the husband had moved into the wife's home, where she and her kids had already lived for over 10 years.

I was helping the wife clear out the rec room, and we created a large pile of her husband's things, which she wanted him to put in the garage. When he came home and saw the pile, it immediately started an argument (which was *very* uncomfortable to be in the middle of, let me tell you!). The wife eventually left and I was alone with the husband (again, *very* uncomfortable), but to my absolute surprise, his eyes started to fill with tears.

"When I moved in here, I got rid of 75% of my stuff," he said. "I think there should be room in this house for the last quarter of my stuff."

Good point.

When we don't make adequate room for our housemates—whether they are children or adults—we send the not-so-subtle message that they are not welcome in the home. In order to make them feel respected, we must establish spaces where they—and their possessions—can reasonably live. We do this by dealing with our own stuff first.

Set an Example

Monkey see, monkey do. And if your house is like mine, you've got a lot of monkeys running around. Let's talk about the big one and the small ones: your spouse and your kids.

Getting the Hubby on Board

Josh is not a minimalist. When I read books about couples who adopt minimalism together, I sigh. How much easier would this be if Josh didn't feel the need to keep a collection of Star Wars toys and baseball cards in the attic? But he's the love of my life and I love him more than I care about those tubs of stuff, so when I started minimizing, I specifically didn't touch his things, and I still don't.

One of my first forays into decluttering involved our bedroom. I remember how I carefully cleared the clutter from my own nightstand and left his completely untouched. (Yes, that was hard!) I also didn't ask him to clean up his nightstand. I just simplified mine, and let his be.

Interestingly, one week later, Josh's mom came to visit and he chose that time to clean up his nightstand. I overheard him say to his mom, "Rose is cleaning up everything in the house. I don't want to look like a slob."

Ah, the power of a positive example!

As the years have gone by, I've noticed how Josh has slowly but surely adopted more minimalist habits—based on my example, not my nagging. (I mean, husbands love nagging, don't they? Just ask them! There's nothing that makes them want to get things done more quickly than a nagging wife, right? As a matter of fact, I think I'll go nag Josh about something right now.)

About a month ago, Josh went to an annual golf outing at work, and received, as usual, the annual swag bag of stuff. Before I adopted minimalism, Josh would have probably just added this stuff to the existing stuff in our house, or worse, tossed the entire bag into the closet to "deal with later," and of course, "later" never comes. But this time he sat down at the kitchen table and immediately unpacked every item in the bag and made decisions.

"Do we need this cooler bag?" he asked. "How about this hat?"

He made piles of donations, and yes, he kept some of the stuff, but that's okay. It's his swag and he can keep what he wants. The important thing is he took the time to decide what that was, as opposed to just adding more stuff to our lives.

Last week we came home from a 10-day vacation where Josh had purchased his favorite souvenir: a pint glass from a local brewery. He has a collection of these glasses in our kitchen and we use them as our daily drinking glasses (for water, not just beer, please don't judge!). As Josh unpacked, he put the pint glass in the cupboard and—without my urging/nagging—chose two other pint glasses to donate.

"We already have two of this kind," he said. "And I didn't even go to the event that's on this one."

See? Making decisions, practicing minimalist habits. These are all things the people in your house can and will do if you set the stage by taking care of your own things.

Teaching Kids to Let Go

Yes, it works with kids, too.

I'll admit, when I first started minimizing, I snuck around behind my kids' backs and donated a heck of a lot of their stuff. I think if kids are under the age of five, this is fine. They are too young to really make decisions about their stuff (especially if there is an overwhelming amount of it, which in my case, there definitely was) and they probably won't notice what's missing.

But as my kids grew and became more aware, I knew I needed to wade into the scary waters of letting them make decisions about their own stuff. This terrified me, mostly because I had no experience minimizing with my kids. Would they cling like crazy to their stuff? Would I damage them irreparably, resulting in high therapy bills later in life?

I'm happy to say that neither of those things happened. (Well, I guess the therapy bills remain to be seen.)

They were five years old and it was about a month before Christmas. My kids, of course, were eagerly anticipating the arrival of Santa and his bag 'o goodies. I decided to use Old Saint Nick to my advantage for our first decluttering session.

"Hey guys, Santa's coming in a few weeks, but there's a problem. He can't bring you new toys unless you give some of your old toys to kids who don't have any. So today we're going to go through your toys and decide what you want to keep and what you can donate or sell."

To my utter surprise, they didn't bat an eyelash and immediately dug into the task of sorting.

Of course, I directed this endeavor, similar to how I help clients. We sorted toys into like-with-like categories first and then dealt with just one category at a time.

It was very interesting to see their choices. I was astounded when my boys ruthlessly halved their Matchbox car collection with reasons like, "He's too slow" and "He doesn't fit on the track." Similarly, I couldn't believe when my daughter chose to keep a hand-me-down, rough-looking Barbie while donating her newer sparkly Cinderella Barbie.

It was hard to watch them minimize some of their toys, especially ones I had just bought them the previous summer for their birthday. However, I felt the exercise was only valuable if I left the choices completely up to them. If they wanted to keep a crappy McDonald's toy, they kept it. If they wanted to let go of the very, very nice wooden barn with wooden animals that I personally loved, but they never played with? Well, okay.

My job as a parent is to teach them decision-making skills and responsibility. What would I teach them if I gave them choices, but then made the decisions for them anyway? (Answer: that mom is in charge of your stuff, not you. Oh, I can visualize the passive-aggressive teenagers this type of parenting would create.)

Of course, there were certain times I stepped in with parameters to help them decide. For example, my daughter had three dollhouses. I lined them up and said she could pick two to keep and one to sell. She chose to keep the two plastic ones and sell the nicer wooden one. This would definitely *not* have been my choice, but again, I wanted her to own the decision, so I simply said, "Okay" and posted the wooden one for sale on my moms group, where it sold like hotcakes. She got the keep the cash, making her one happy 5-year-old.

At the end of that first de-cluttering session, we had two shopping bags full of minimized toys. I believe my son Reese said it best: "Santa's going to bring us LOTS of toys now!" Of course, I would have preferred a more altruistic, "So many kids are going to be happy to play with these toys now!" response, but you know what? He was five, and when you're five, Santa's a pretty big deal.

Minimizing with my kids helped me in two ways. First, I felt relieved that we'd cleared space for the new stuff headed their way in December. But secondly, and more importantly, I knew that my kids were fully capable of making the decisions necessary to keep their possessions in check. I didn't need to stress about it.

If the number of toys ever became too much, we could tackle the problem together. It's like that "teach a man to fish" saying, except with stuff: "De-clutter *for* your kids, find peace for a day. De-clutter *with* your kids, find peace for a lifetime."

Of course, that first decluttering session was just one of many that followed. We still do big minimizing sessions before their birthday and Christmas, but most of our donating happens as stuff slowly trickles in throughout the year, which, even when you're a minimalist, happens.

My kids are used to me saying things like, "I see your babysitter bought you all new toys for being so good. That's awesome! Do you think you could each find a toy to donate to a kid who doesn't have any?"

Usually they can. But sometimes they can't. And that's okay. I try hard to approach my kids with questions, not commands. "Do you think you could …" is an invitation, an offer, not an expectation. There are times my kids have said no, they can't find anything to donate. It's not easy for me to smile in response and say, "Okay. Maybe next time." But I do it, because I want to teach my kids a skill, not engender resentment. Which, by the way, is a very real risk if our kids are over the age of five and we sneak around behind their backs and donate things when they're not looking.

Purgatory

Now before you think you have to ask your kid about every little tchotchke and trinket they bring home, please realize that I do have one exception to the "Involve Your Kids" rule. I call it Purgatory.

If you walked into my kitchen and looked at the top of my fridge, you would see an innocent-looking green bin. You'd probably think, "Oh, Rose is a minimalism and simplicity coach. I bet that green bin contains some neatly stacked tea towels or binders full of color-coded weekly meal plans." If you got really curious and climbed on a step stool to look, you might be surprised to see: a mess of papers, trinkets, and the like.

But this is no random "I-don't-know-where-to-put-this-so-I'll-put-it-here" kind of mess. This mess contains very specific items for a very specific purpose: Purgatory.

Let me explain. My kids constantly acquire "prizes" from school and sports and the dentist and birthday parties and other kids. These items very quickly add clutter to the house. I've observed that my kids consider these prizes awesome for about T minus 2 minutes, at which point they leave said prizes to linger on the kitchen counter like forgotten shipwreck victims.

Purgatory is my approach to this dilemma. It's the holding tank for items that aren't "good" enough to be put into the toy rotation nor "bad" enough to be thrown away immediately. They need a testing ground, a place to prove whether or not they are worthy enough to be remembered. The testing ground is the top of my fridge. Anything put in the bin stays there until I either empty it—which I do whenever it is full—or a little person asks about an item and I retrieve it.

You may have a few questions, such as:

Isn't this sneaky? Yes, it is. But if you are a parent, you know that our #1 job is to cleverly, yet harmlessly, deceive our children. I'm joking, but not totally joking. Consider the Easter bunny, the tooth fairy, Santa, that dang Elf. We do it all the time. This is really no different.

Can I do this with all the items my child acquires? Nope. Then the jig would be up. Pick your Purgatory items carefully. Think fast food toys, coloring pages, certificates of achievement from online math games. These are the types of items kids forget about quickly.

But I thought you just said we should let kids choose what to do with their stuff? Aren't you being a hypocrite? You are right, I did say we should allow kids to make decisions about their own stuff. However, decision fatigue sets in when we ask kids to make decisions about every little thing they own. Allow your kids to make decisions about bigger, more important items— birthday gifts, crafts that required several days to make, memorabilia they purchased with their own money—but it's okay to save them (and yourself) the hassle when it comes to the small stuff.

What if my kid asks about an item in Purgatory and it's already been sent to, you know, it's final destination? Again, fall back on your #1 parenting skill: clever but harmless deception. A simple, "I don't know where that is, honey," is an honest answer. *Do* you know where the trash man took last week's trash? I'm guessing not. And if your kid regularly asks about Purgatory items, you need to scale back your Purgatory zeal a bit.

What types of items can I put in Purgatory? Items regularly found in our Purgatory include:

- **Prizes from school/activities.**

- **Items from birthday treat bags.** Consider this my humble plea to all fellow parents that we unite and just stop with the birthday treat bags. Really, is there any "treat" in plastic trinkets that clutter our homes and eventually end up in a landfill? I think not.

- **Drawings my kids give me that aren't special enough to put in my memorabilia box.** Yes, it hurts to say it, but it is true. Not every sticky note with "I love you" gets saved forever. I can't save everything or nothing is truly special.

- **Small crafts**

Do your kids ever ask why you put stuff on top of the fridge? Never, which surprises me. I add stuff to and retrieve stuff from Purgatory right in front of them, and they've never asked about it.

How often do your kids ask for items that you've put in Purgatory? I've observed a 98/2 rule: 98% of Purgatory items are never asked about again. And of the 2% they do ask about, I'm able to produce them 98% of the time. I'd say I'm winning with these stats.

Purgatory is a simple, practical way to deal with all the little stuff so you can spend more of your time seriously decluttering the bigger stuff.

In Brief

I urge you, be the example in your home and keep your mouth shut (taped, if you need to!) about any clutter for which your spouse and kids are responsible. Not only will they feel immensely respected, but they just might surprise you by following your lead. Nobody likes to be nagged to clean up their stuff, especially if the nagger has quite a pile of her own to deal with. This is hypocritical and even your kids can see that.

Think of a pebble dropped in a pond. You want to be that pebble, affecting your own areas first, then gradually allowing your influence and positive example to affect those you live with. I promise, it will.

Are you ready to get started? Great!

The next three chapters show how you can apply the LESS Method™ to three different areas of your home: your bedroom, bathroom, and kitchen. I chose these areas because they are probably under your jurisdiction, so they're good places to start.

Also, I want you to build your minimizing chops in spaces you feel comfortable so you can tackle the other areas of your home like a minimizing champ. The cool thing about using this system to declutter is that the approach really doesn't change from space to space. The way I approach a closet is the same way I approach a garage and the same way I approach a craft room.

Practice your skills in spaces you control first, and you will be a pro by the time you venture out to other areas of your house!

Think About It

What is one area of your home that is completely under your jurisdiction?

What would happen if you decluttered just this one space?

How would it feel to not have to nag your spouse or kids to clean up?

What would happen if you involved your kids in the decluttering process and allowed them to make decisions about their own stuff?

CHAPTER 8

Your Bedroom: Lessons Learned on Clothes Mountain

"It almost makes you sick, doesn't it?" Sarah said as she surveyed the mountain of clothing still heaped on her bed. We were about halfway through our first session, working our way through her large walk-in closet. We had already donated eight trash bags of clothing and still hadn't addressed her second closet, which was in the guest room.

She sighed, eyeing the pile of colorful tops, dresses, and slacks, many with tags still on.

"It's just such a waste."

I couldn't have said it better.

Americans love clothing. And we own lots of it. So much, in fact, that the Council for Textile Recycling estimates that the average American ends up throwing away 70 pounds of clothing and textiles per year.

One image of clothing excess that always sticks out in my mind comes from a visit to the Goodwill outlet here in Dayton. It is essentially the end-of-the-line for our local Goodwill stores' unsold clothing and goods.

My guide showed me the baler, a massive machine that bundles unsold clothing into large rectangular blocks. These blocks are then sold by the pound to salvage companies who either use them to create rags and recycled products, such as insulation, or ship them to third world countries. (Ever wonder why those kids in needy countries have Pepsi T-shirts? Now you know.)

As I stood next to the shoulder-high bales of clothing, I had two thoughts: 1) Deep gratitude to Goodwill for keeping these items out of landfills for a while, and 2) We all buy way too much clothing.

With this in mind, your clothing is an excellent place to start honing your minimalism skills. It is 100% under your jurisdiction, and you probably own tons of it.

Like all areas of your home, we'll apply the LESS Method™ to get this job done.

Step 1: Lay Out Your Vision & Purpose

Step inside your closet and survey your surroundings for a moment. Try to notice without judging. Just observe. Are the hangers bunched together? Is there dust on the shoulders of some of those suits? Do wild, pairless shoes roam the floor like unsupervised toddlers at a fast food play place?

Now close your eyes. Imagine that your closet looks perfect, exactly the way you want it to be. What do you see? This, friends, is your **VISION**. Grab that marker and paper, write it down, and tape it up.

Next question: "What is the purpose of your clothing?"

Clients always look at me a little strangely when I ask this question. I mean, isn't the ultimate purpose of clothing to protect us from the elements and, more importantly, arrest? (The latter, of course, doesn't apply if you live in certain "open-minded" communities, in which case, you've probably got the minimal clothing thing down and can just skip this chapter. Just be sure to put on sunscreen.)

But when I ask this question, what I want to know is: *What are the different spheres of your life? Or, what are the different roles you fulfill and how do you need to dress for those roles?*

This is important information, because the roles we play determine the clothes we wear.

For example, one of my clients is a young dad who works at a guitar store. When I asked him about the spheres of his life and how he needed to dress for them, we came up with this list:

- **Guitar store:** company T-shirts and jeans

- **Home:** casual clothes for relaxing or working around the house

- **Exercise:** running shorts and T-shirts

- **Dress-up:** Occasional special events

After we made this list, I knew that this client needed a wardrobe that focused mainly on relaxing clothing. His work environment has a uniform and outside of work, he spends most of his time at home, exercising or hanging out with his family. Since he doesn't attend many dress-up events, one nice suit and a couple of ties would suffice. We wrote down his list and taped it up to keep us focused as we worked.

Laying out your vision and purpose is an important step when addressing clothing because many of us own clothes that don't reflect our lives. I've been in the closets of stay-at-home parents where 80% of the clothing is business attire. I've also seen clients who own almost nothing but clothes for cleaning the house, when they actually lead professional lives outside the home.

You want to make sure your clothing reflects the roles you need to play and the best way to do that is to grab another sheet of blank paper and write down every **PURPOSE** your clothing needs to serve. There should be more than one. Tape that sucker to the closet door. Now that you've got the end game in sight, it's time to execute.

Step 2: Empty

"I don't have that many clothes because I hate shopping," Becky said confidently. I nodded, keeping my mouth shut as I emptied the contents of her closet and drawers onto her bed. Becky has been my best friend since high school, and

I was thrilled to help her minimize her wardrobe on this glorious, kid-free Saturday afternoon.

When we finally had every single sock, shirt, and skirt heaped on her bed, Becky cocked her head at the pile we'd created.

"Huh. I guess I have more clothes than I thought."

This is a common reaction when we see how many clothes we own. Most of us own way more clothing than we think, and much more than we could ever wear.

Emptying the entire contents of your wardrobe might feel a bit overwhelming, but it is the only way to get a handle on the entirety of your clothing collection. I always recommend using your bed as the landing pad for "clothes mountain," since you will be forced to make decisions on all that clothing if you want to sleep that night.

If you have several closets worth of clothing, do one bed-full at a time. Remember, it's perfectly fine to minimize in chunks. You can even split your minimizing up by type: T-shirts one day, sweaters the next, and so on. It really doesn't matter how you do it, what's most important is that you start.

Step 3: Sort It Twice

1st: Like-with-Like

Do your first sort as you put your clothing on your bed: pants together, dresses together, and so on. Most of us have our clothing organized this way already, so this should be easy.

2nd: Decide

Take a moment to review your VISION and PURPOSE signs. Remember, *the roles we play determine the clothes we wear.* Keeping your purpose in mind will keep you focused.

The good news is, I've found that clothing is one of the easiest categories to make decisions about, which is why it's a good place to start. Look at each item and make the quickest "Yes" or "No" decision you can. "Yes" means it suits your purpose and "No" means it doesn't and should go to someone else. Keep your white trash bags handy for all those donations—there will be a lot!

Of course, some items give us pause and there isn't an easy Yes or No. If you get stuck, here are some questions to help you:

- Have I worn it in the last year?

- Even if I have worn it recently, did I *feel good* wearing it?

- Would I reach for this item in a group of similar items? (For example, if it's a sweater, would I grab this sweater over the others in my closet?)

- Does it fit my body well? (No scrunching, bunching, stretching, etc. Do I spend all day tugging it up or down?)

- Is it in good condition, free from stains, tears, missing buttons, etc.?

Sometimes clients come across clothing they are reluctant to part with because the item cost a significant amount of money and hasn't been worn much, if at all. I usually point out that this item is not earning them any money by sitting in their closet, and I also ask: *Would you spend that same amount of money to purchase it again?* If not, we both know the item would better serve someone else.

As you sort, keep a list of items you need to buy. (Yes, this minimalist is recommending you go shopping!) When I help clients with their closets, we almost always find "holes" in their wardrobes, usually related to basics like good jeans and quality T-shirts. Basics are the backbone of any good wardrobe, and if you're lacking, now is the time to invest.

It may help to have a good, honest friend by your side as you do this. Not only does a friend make the process more fun, but outside eyes can often see things we can't.

I loved helping Becky simplify her wardrobe that Saturday afternoon; she ended up donating about 80% of her clothing, which is not unusual. And as she tried on some of her "maybe" items, I noticed that certain colors (greens and blues) looked great on her, while others (yellows, specifically) did not. This helped her make better decisions about what she should keep and donate.

At the end of our session, we headed to the mall for some focused, laughter-filled shopping to replenish the basics in her closet. She went to work confidently that week, knowing she looked (and more importantly, felt) fabulous.

Step 4: Systemize

Congrats! Your closet should look slimmed down and beautiful right about now! Remember to get those donations to your car, put any memorabilia items in a separate spot, and relocate Elsewhere items. Now let's talk about how to maintain this minimized closet system.

First and foremost, remember the power of your two maintenance habits: the constant donation box and the one in/one out rule. These habits are crucial to keeping clothes, especially, in check. I keep my donation box on the floor of my closet just for this reason. I've donated a shirt that I'd worn no more than a week prior, when I suddenly realized, *I don't like the way this fits me.* Into the box it goes.

When I buy a new item of clothing, I put an old one into the box. At the end of the season, when I'm rotating my capsule wardrobe, I put in anything I didn't wear in the last three months. And so it goes. My wardrobe stays fresh, small, and seasonable, and I never have to do a big "clothes mountain" purge ever again.

A Word on Capsule Wardrobes

If you Google "capsule wardrobe" you'll find many enlightening articles written by more fashionable people than me. I encourage you to do this. My favorite capsule wardrobe expert is Courtney Carver. You can find her online at Project333.com.

But I'll give you a layman's definition: a capsule wardrobe is a seasonal wardrobe of roughly 20-40 pieces. A "piece" is one item of clothing, such as a shirt or pair of pants.

If you really want to keep a minimal wardrobe, I don't know of a better way to do it than to create a capsule wardrobe. My fashionable friend Nessa helped me make one two years ago and I will never go back. You can read all about my experience creating my first capsule on my blog at RoseLounsbury.com.

The easiest way to create a capsule wardrobe is to remove everything from your closet that is not appropriate for the current season, so your only visible options for getting dressed are seasonable items. Put your off-season items in storage somewhere else in your house.

You dress solely from these in-season items for about three months, until the season changes. Then you rotate some items out and some others in, maintaining your 20-40 pieces. For example, I wear my "summer" wardrobe from June-August, then I switch to my "fall" wardrobe in September. Three months later, I switch to winter, and then to spring. This regular, seasonal appraisal forces me to donate as I go, stock up on good basics, dress deliberately, and actually look like I have a sense of style. In short, I dress better.

One note: your 20-40 pieces does NOT include underwear (keep as much of that as you want) or anything you would wear exclusively for sleep or exercise. Nessa helped me differentiate between "loungewear" (aka the mom uniform of yoga pants and a sweatshirt) and the type of clothing I should wear to "get dressed" for the day.

This was a huge eye-opener for me! Before doing a capsule, I never really "got dressed" but spent most of my days looking like I was about to hit up a spinning class. I now put my sleep and exercise clothes in my dresser and leave my closet free of everything except my capsule. When I "get dressed" for the day, I go to my closet, NOT the dresser (except for the underwear, that's important). This forces me to dress better.

That might sound difficult, but if you have kids, you already probably do this for them. Most of us rotate our children's clothing seasonally, so if you think about it, you could easily create a capsule wardrobe, following the same principles you use in your kids' closets.

A Word on Body Image

Ladies, let's talk about body image for a moment, shall we? Many of us avoid dealing with our wardrobes due to negative thoughts about how we look. This jiggles, that sticks out further than it used to, and those are engaged in a slow Southern migration that shows no sign of stopping. I could write a whole book about why we do this to ourselves, but let's suffice it to say that our culture judges women's appearance more harshly than men's. Add to this the fact that many of us undergo the hostile body takeover called pregnancy a time or two during our lives, and it makes sense that we have a tough time dealing with our clothing.

Many of us have felt the urge to hold on to clothing for "when I lose the weight." I do not encourage this. (My only exception to this rule is if you have had a baby within the last year.) There are several reasons for this. First, often the clothing we want to fit back into is outdated. Are you really going to bust out that backless shirt from college when you lose the last 10 pounds?

Let me tell you this: *When you lose that weight, you owe it to yourself to buy new clothing that you will love.* After all, buying new clothes in a smaller size is the best reward for losing weight.

Second, and more important, I think it is psychologically damaging to have a closet full of clothes you can't fit into. No one could look at a closet full of too-skinny jeans and Lycra belly shirts and feel good about themselves. (If this is what your closet actually looks like—and you don't moonlight as a go-go dancer—please call me immediately for fashion intervention.) And if you allow yourself to feel defeated by your clothing on a daily basis, how do you expect to lose weight?

You're killing your self-esteem every time you open that closet. Keep your confidence high, and get that clothing out of your sight and into the hands of someone else who can use it now. I'm sure there is a houseful of sorority sisters somewhere who needs those Lycra belly shirts more than you do.

In short, wear the best clothes you can, at the size you currently are, and when the time comes, you can happily trade them in for a smaller size.

Last, and most importantly, why don't we all do a good thing for the world and just love ourselves a bit more? Our bodies do amazing things for us every day. They allow us to walk, hug our kids, bake lasagna, and even pull those annoying dried clumps of Play-Doh out of the carpet. Many of us can also thank our bodies for the gift of our beautiful children. We should be grateful for every stretch mark and extra jiggle. Namaste.

A Word on Fashion

Ah, women's fashion, the mercurial beast. I often sigh with envy when I look at Josh's work wardrobe: dark suits, light shirts, and a few ties of different colors. How easy would it be to get dressed everyday if nearly all the decisions were already made for you?

Alas, women's wardrobes are much more complicated than our male counterparts, resulting in more decisions and—often—a less polished look. When it comes to getting dressed, I think we would do well to take a few lessons from the dudes. I'm not making an argument for the return of the 1980s power shoulder pads, (although, if you like that look, rock it, girlfriend) but I think we could apply some lessons from menswear the world of women's fashion.

Rule #1: Basics. Men's wardrobes often look more polished than women's wardrobes because they rely heavily on basics: dark suits, light shirts, a pop of color with a nice tie. No man looks bad dressed like this. Nearly all of my female clients are lacking basics in their wardrobe. I suggest having an 80/20 rule for style, meaning 80% of your wardrobe should be basics (nice jeans, versatile dresses and skirts, crisp white tees, etc.) and 20% should be flair (colorful scarves, animal print, a statement jacket, etc.).

This 80/20 rule allows you to still be fashionable, but because it rests solidly on basics, you don't have to regularly buy the "newest trend" each season.

Rule #2: Wear what YOU like. I used to think that having a nice wardrobe meant I had to follow every "Top 10 Must-Haves for your Spring Wardrobe" list that I found online. This is not true. There is no hard and fast rule for what looks good on everyone. Find the looks that work for you and work them.

For example, I used to keep a white button-down shirt, black dress slacks, and khakis in my closet because I read somewhere that those were staples of a classic wardrobe. The only problem? I don't like wearing white button-down shirts, black slacks or khakis. I like comfortable, blousy dresses that I can dress up or dress down. These are my "basics" which you will not find on any of those Internet lists. I encourage you to look at your wardrobe and really examine the clothes YOU like and feel good in. These are your basics. Build off of them.

In Brief

Most of us are hanging on to excess clothing that is outdated, ill-fitting, or simply not our style. Take this time to free yourself of items that no longer fit your body or your life, and allow that clothing to be of use to someone *now*.

Think About It:

Are you hanging on to clothing that reflects a past time in your life? What would happen if you let it go?

Are you hanging on to clothing that doesn't fit your body or personality well? If so, what is keeping you from wearing clothes you like?

Does your closet lack basics?

How could others in your community benefit from your excess clothing?

What would it feel like to have a smaller, seasonal wardrobe that fit you well?

CHAPTER 9

Your Bathroom:
Looking Good, Girl

I have two truths for you: 1) You are already beautiful, and 2) You are probably clean, most of the time. If you don't believe the first, you are doing yourself, your loved ones, and the world at large a great disservice. Please acknowledge and add a little more happy to the planet. And the second is most definitely true, unless you are living in the fifteenth century. In which case, how are you reading this? And please tell everyone about the awesomeness of hand-washing and vaccines.

Now that you understand that you are beautiful and clean, this third truth will make a lot of sense: *You have way too many beauty products in your bathroom.*

That's right, the next stop on our decluttering journey is the bathroom, an area that—like your closet—is probably 100% under your jurisdiction. It's also probably crammed with a bunch of stuff you don't need.

Again, we will apply the LESS Method™ to help you get that beauty clutter under control.

Step 1: Lay Out Your Vision & Purpose

My bathroom shelves used to resemble a Clinique counter clearance sale that had lasted since 1995. If you feel me on that, it's time to get to work. First, take a moment to envision your perfect bathroom. Perhaps it would look something like a hotel, with clear countertops and minimal visible products. Imagine how much easier it would be for you to get ready in a bathroom like this.

Got the **VISION**? Good. Write it down on some paper and tape it up. Now let's talk about your beauty MO.

Spend a moment miming your normal cleansing and beauty routine. It might seem silly, but this is what I do every time I pack for a trip to make sure I take the right products. I mime showering, putting on lotion, doing my hair, and putting on makeup.

Now, take a glance at the products in your bathroom. Do they reflect the actions you just mimed? Or are there superfluous amounts of bottles and potions littering your shelves?

Jot down the basic steps of your beauty routine. This is your **PURPOSE** statement. This list will be your go-to guide as you declutter this space.

Step 2: Empty

You know the drill by now—everything out! Empty your shelves and cupboards of every last shampoo and sample of free moisturizer. No one is spared your scrutiny today. As you empty, check for grossness. By this I mean products that are leaky, clumpy, or funky. Toss these easy "No's" in the trash as you go.

Step 3: Sort It Twice

1st Sort: Like with Like

Line 'em up. Lotions with lotions, lipsticks with lipsticks, body glitter with body glitter. (Hey, how did that body glitter already escape the trash? If you aren't planning to attend a junior high dance in the near future, that needs to be tossed, STAT.) I love this step because you quickly start seeing the excess, making decisions oh-so-much easier.

2nd Sort: Decide

Now it's time to sort the men from the boys, or, if you prefer, the lash pumpers from lash clumpers. I recommend you sort into just two piles: Keep and Trash. With beauty products, you really don't need Donate, Sell, or Elsewhere piles. Most charities won't take opened products and you really don't want to be that person on your Buy/Sell/Trade group who's trying to sell a half-used jar of salt scrub. And as far as Elsewhere goes, where else would you use beauty products except in your bathroom? (Okay, maybe one or two things in your purse, but that's it!)

Unless you have a good friend who you know truly wants your unwanted products, stick with tossing your unloved ones in the trash, and remember this day the next time you're in the beauty aisle. You really should only buy products you already know you love.

I'll admit, this can be hard. I, too, used to harbor unloved and unused beauty products, hoping against hope that I would someday discover their magic and be transformed into the flawless-faced damsel on the packaging. If you also feel this urge, please refer to Truth #1: *You are already beautiful.*

But the truth is, some beauty products work. Some don't. Save yourself some grief and cash and just stick with what works for you. That means ditching a heck of a lot of stuff in your bathroom. And don't give in to that "But I don't want to waste it!" excuse. *If it is sitting unused in your cupboard, it is currently being wasted.* Let it go and be grateful for the new space in which to house products you truly love.

The same principle applies to medicines. You should only keep medications that you are currently taking, as well as a reasonably-sized stock for basic first aid, upset tummies, and headaches. You don't need 15 different kinds of pain relievers or five flavors of cough syrup.

Check the dates on everything. I'd wager a bet that many of your medications are past their expiration date. If you find old prescription medications, please, please don't flush these down the toilet or put them in the trash. I like drinking drug-free water, don't you? Visit dea.gov to find out when the next prescription drug take back day is in your community. If this date is too far off, call your local pharmacy to find out if they offer a program for disposing of old meds. It might cost a small fee, but that is much better than polluting everyone's drinking water.

How Long to Keep Makeup

We all know that makeup expires, but when, exactly? According to WebMD, here's how long you should keep makeup:

- **Mascara & liquid eyeliner** – No more than 4 months
- **Liquid foundation** – Up to 1 year
- **Lip gloss** – 6 months
- **Lipstick** – 1 year
- **Powders** – Up to 2 years

It's safe to say that if you can't remember when you bought it, it needs to go. To avoid this in the future, keep a marker in your makeup bag to write the purchase date on your packaging. Be ruthless, be focused, and above all, keep that vision of your perfect bathroom in mind to inspire you!

Step 4: Systemize

Alright! Your shelves should be breathing easy by now. As you put your favorite products back in their newly decluttered space, group them by degree of use. Keep your daily use products (face wash, deodorant, daily meds, etc.) nearby and your infrequently used products (travel-sized items, rarely used medicines) farther away. You should be able to reach any product you use regularly without taking a single step from your sink.

To maintain your streamlined beauty routine, follow the one in/one out rule. When you get a new mascara, let the old one go. And be serious about whether or not new products work for you. Like most women, I like to try new products sometimes, but if I try something and hate it, I toss it quickly. I'm not going to start liking it more if it sits on my shelves for eight months.

A Complete List of My Products

To give you some decluttering inspiration, here's a list of every beauty and personal care product I use. So, if you are curious about what makes the magic happen, read on.

In the Shower

- Shampoo

- Conditioner

- Soap

That's it. If you have more than this in your shower, I'm not really sure what you're washing. But hey, let me know, because maybe I should be washing that, too!

Teeth

- Toothpaste

- Floss

I really don't think these need any more explanation.

Body Care

- Scented lotion

- Vaseline

- Deodorant

I use scented lotion because I don't like perfume, and Vaseline is my own personal tiger balm. The deodorant is self-explanatory. (Unless you live in the aforementioned fifteenth century, in which case, add this to the list of things you need to tell folks about.)

For a Clean Face

- Face wash

- Moisturizer

- Eye cream

- Night cream

Yes, my face care products are a bit more numerous, but hey, a girl's gotta protect the money maker.

For a Made-Up Face

- Foundation

- Blush

- Mascara

- Eye shadow

- Eyeliner

- Tinted lip balm

I definitely don't wear all this make-up every day. I think most ladies look better with minimal make-up, and their significant others would probably agree! But I wanted to let you know the extent of my supply. I have about one container of each of the above, and on a daily basis, I wear just the foundation, blush, and mascara. I add the eye shadow, eyeliner and the tinted lip balm for a hot night out on the town, such as going to Kroger after 9pm.

Hair

- Hair oil

- Dry shampoo

- Hairspray

My curly hair needs moisture, hence the oil, and dry shampoo is like a little can of follicle magic for second-day hair. I also keep some good old-fashioned hairspray on hand, because my stylish sister, who knows about these things, says hairspray is the #1 most underused beauty product in America. Dolly Parton would agree. And who argues with Dolly Parton? Nobody.

And that's it. All the beauty magic in my arsenal. With these products, I feel clean, beautiful, and ready to hit the town. Look out, Kroger. I've got coupons.

Think About It:

Could you simplify your beauty routine by using less products?

What would it feel like to have a clean, decluttered bathroom with just your favorite, daily-use products at your fingertips?

What would happen if you let go of all the products you don't absolutely love?

CHAPTER 10

Your Kitchen: What's Cooking in All That Clutter?

I remember reading my first book about minimalism, oh so many years ago. I got to about chapter 3, set the book down, and immediately went to my kitchen and started pulling things out of the cupboard. I donated five boxes worth of excess kitchen stuff that day, and I thought, "Wow! I'm done! Perfect!"

But the strange thing is, as the years have gone by, I've continued to return to my kitchen, decluttering items here and there as I notice I no longer use them. That's the thing about minimalism: as you learn to live with less, you learn that you can live with even less than you had originally thought.

So, the kitchen is an excellent third stop on your decluttering journey, because—unless you don't eat food and therefore never prepare food—you probably have some say in what is stored here.

Note: if you share cooking duties with someone else in your home, you MUST involve them in this process. In my own home, I do the weekday cooking and Josh takes care of the weekends, so I can't get away with decluttering the kitchen without his input. I learned this the hard way after I once tried to sneakily declutter a cast iron pan behind Josh's back. It did not end well. You can read about it on my blog.

So, if you share cooking duties with someone else, now's a good time to bring them along for the ride. You've got some decluttering experience, your pebble is starting to make ripples in the pond, and this is a great time to get the family involved. And you might be surprised how much more fun decluttering is with a buddy!

The LESS Method™ really works in the kitchen, so let's follow the steps to tame this breeding ground of excessive utensils and cookware.

Step 1: Lay Out Your Vision and Purpose

What do you want your kitchen to look like? Do you desire clear countertops, easy-to-locate dishware, and utensil drawers that don't resemble the cluttered castoffs from a medieval torture chamber? Write down your **VISION** and tape it up.

Then, even more importantly, think about **PURPOSE**. I know, you're saying, "Duh, Rose! The purpose is to cook stuff!" Really? Is that all? Do you use your kitchen for other things? Is it the place you pay bills, help kids with homework, or charge your phones? Kitchens are always the heart of the home and I've found that this room usually serves more purposes than any other. Think of all the things you *do* in this room and write them down. Tape this next to your vision.

Step 2: Empty

This is the fun part! Get it all out, every last thing. If your kitchen is large or you feel overwhelmed, start at the door and move clockwise, top-to-bottom, left-to-right, one drawer and cupboard at a time.

Step 3: Sort It Twice

1st Sort: Like-with-Like

This is so, so important in the kitchen. I've often found that people have similar types of items in many different parts of their kitchens and they don't realize it until we take it all out and put everybody with their buddies. Do you have spatulas in multiple drawers? Baking dishes in four different cupboards? Get them all out. It's time to take stock.

Typical like-with-like categories found in a kitchen include:

- Dishes
- Bowls
- Mugs
- Cups
- Wine glasses
- Kid dishes
- Silverware

- Utensils
- Pans
- Bakeware
- Food storage
- Small appliances
- Randoms
- Memorabilia

Like I said, these are typical categories, but you should create the categories that naturally emerge from your own kitchen. It really doesn't matter what categories you use, as long as you have all like items together. And to really get a handle on your kitchen you will probably need to subdivide these categories a bit. I've found that most people have enough utensils to equip an at-capacity cooking school. Get all your spatulas, wooden spoons, and vegetable peelers with their like-minded brethren. You want to be able to compare apples-to-apples as much as possible.

Note: You will inevitably find things that are not utensils or dishes: photos, coupons, junk mail, spare change, random cords to who-knows-what. If you're not careful, this miscellaneous stuff, probably from your junk drawer (or drawers, let's be honest) will throw you for a loop and grind your minimizing process to a screeching halt. I recommend treating your junk drawer as its own space and sorting it separately. I'll address that at the end of this chapter.

2nd Sort: Decide

Alright! You've got your ducks in a row and now it's time to select the best ducks. Before we do that, though, take a look at your hands. How many do you have? Unless you've been the lucky recipient of a nuclear waste accident that left you with extra appendages and Spidey-sense, you probably have two. Keep that in mind.

Now I want you to imagine it's a Friday in middle school gym class. You know what that means: dodgeball day. Aka: self-esteem reduction day. Now imagine that you are the coolest kid in the class, the star pitcher of the baseball team. Your name is Chad or Chaz or Chet. No one really knows, and it doesn't matter. You're awesome. And you're about the kick some can.

Naturally, your underpaid, weekend-focused gym teacher has made you team captain and it's time to pick your favorites. The guys who are going to get the job done. The ones who are going to help you cream the other team. To accomplish this, you must choose the strongest, the best, the most ruthless. The ones who won't feel bad about nailing the band kid square in the back with a dodgeball sent at light speed.

Okay … I might need to back off this metaphor a bit. I'm starting to get some PTSD-like shakes. (In real life, I may or may not have been band kid.)

Let's bring it back to decluttering: *you are the team captain of your kitchen and you need to pick the best tools for the job.* Remember: *you only have two hands.* How many wooden spoons can you actually use at once? Two, if you're extremely dexterous. (Which, if you're Chad/Chaz/Chet, you probably are.)

If you only have four burners on your stove, how many pans can you actually use at once? If you have one oven with two racks, how many sheets of cookies could you possibly be baking at the same time? Let the simple laws of physics guide you as you decide what you *need*—and more importantly, *can use*—in your kitchen.

To give you some context, at my house, we have two wooden spoons: a round one for sweets and a flat one for savories. Everyone in my house has two hands, and we are rarely in the position where more than one person is stirring something at a time, and if we are, a spatula or metal spoon can pinch hit. So, two wooden spoons is the perfect number for us.

So, pick your best, your brightest, your most stir and scrape-worthy, your best bakers and super sauté-ers, and donate the rest. Why? Because you don't need them. They are cluttering your life and your kitchen. They are preventing you from using the absolute best tool for the job. They are the weakest link in your dodgeball game. Remember, you are Chet. It is Friday. And you get to decide who wins this game.

Be the boss and sort everything into these categories:

- Keep
- Donate
- Trash
- Elsewhere
- Sell

You got this, girl.

Step 4: Systemize

If you have reached step four, I want you to flap the covers of this book open and closed a few times right now. That's me clapping for you. You're doing awesome!

It's time to get those donations to the car, take out your trash, post any sellable items online, redistribute your Elsewhere items to their proper homes, and tote all that memorabilia to a separate location to be dealt with later.

Now you have the happy task of putting your treasures back in your empty cupboards. Call me a dork, but I love this part! It's amazing to see how much more space you have. Try leaving a little space between your items as you put them back. Cramming your dishes and glasses shoulder-to-shoulder will make your cupboards look cluttered, even if they are not. Allow them to breathe. Ah! I'm feeling calmer just thinking about it!

This is also the time to put things into bins or containers, if it makes sense. Food storage lids, for example, often stay together better if they are corralled in some type of container. Label, if you need to, so that everybody understands where things go. Remember, you are trying to establish clear "homes" for everything to be easily put back, and that will not happen if the only person who understands your system is you.

Make it obvious to everyone you live with where stuff goes. Remember the couple whose kitchen cupboards I labeled with painter's tape? It might seem ridiculous to have blue tape all over your kitchen with labels like "rolling pin," "cookie sheets," and "CrockPot," but I guarantee no one will put something away in the wrong place if you do that! I once used painter's tape to label my trash and recycling bins, because I was tired of digging sandwich crusts out of the recycling. I always thought I'd upgrade my system someday, but lo-and-behold, if you came to my house today, you'd find those blue labels still in place, still working.

Think about any other systems you need and whether a label would help. Remember the two wooden spoons at my house? Despite my very logical sweet/savory division, Josh used to constantly ask me, "Which spoon is which again?" And I told him the no-duh answer, "The round one is for sweets because if you eat too many sweets, you get rounder." Then he would respond with something like, "But you could get round from eating savories, too, like bacon."

While I disagreed with his obviously flawed logic, I eventually got tired of stirring cookie dough with a spoon reminiscent of last night's stir fry and labeled the handle of each spoon with a skinny Sharpie. Problem solved. Remember, if you live with other people, the system must be painfully obvious to everyone if it is going to be maintained. Do whatever it takes to make it easy on you and your loved ones to keep your kitchen clutter-free.

And speaking of maintenance, would it help to have a constant donation box in your kitchen? I'm guessing you spend a lot of time in there and it might be helpful to have that box ever-available so you can just toss in donations and one in/one out items while drinking your morning coffee. Keeping a donation box in this central part of the house will encourage your housemates to keep donating, as well.

A Word on Junk Drawers

The junk drawer (or drawers, let's be real) is almost always found in the kitchen. People shun the term "junk drawer" but I actually like it. Sure, you could say "utility drawer," but then no one would really know what you're talking about. Junk drawers are one of those common denominators in human culture; they unite us and help us see past our differences. Sure, we may have different religions, skin colors, and customs, but we all have drawers full of mystery cords and pennies. I think we could forge world peace based on that alone.

Of course I'm joking, but the truth is: we all need some sort of drawer for the little stuff, whatever that little stuff may be. For me, it's sticky notes, scissors, rubber bands, and my checkbook. For you it might be your phone charger, hand sanitizer, and an all-access pass to your local history of dental hygiene museum. (Hey, I don't know you. And I don't judge you. But I know your drawer, my brother.) It really doesn't matter what you keep in your junk drawer, but it matters that you use the stuff.

I teach a class on minimalism where I ask a volunteer to sort a junk drawer live. I pack a bin with all sorts of random stuff and let them at it. It's interesting to see how the audience gets involved, shouting, "Trash! That receipt is trash!" or "Put that screwdriver in the garage!" It's like *The Price is Right* except the winner ends up with a drawer of paper clips and pens, not a new car. No one has ever sorted the junk drawer the same way. Each person keeps only the items that suit their personal purpose.

So, keep a junk drawer, but make sure it works for you. Treat it like any other space and follow the LESS Method™ to lay out your vision and purpose, empty, sort, and systemize this drawer. And hey, the next time you meet someone who seems really different than you, remember, you have something very important in common—that drawer in your kitchens.

In Brief

You spend too much time in your kitchen to let it be in a state of cluttered chaos. The kitchen is family central. It's where we gather, connect, swap stories, and reminisce. It's where Aunt Marge burned the turkey one fateful Thanksgiving and you will lovingly rehash the story for many Thanksgivings to come. This space it too important not to simplify. Letting go of your kitchen excess will allow you the freedom to focus on the most important things found in this space: those people you love.

Think About It

What excess items in your kitchen are getting in the way of you living your daily life?

How would it feel to have just what you need and love in your kitchen?

Would a cleaner kitchen improve your family life in any way?

CHAPTER 11

Yeah, But ... What About Paper?

I hope by now you're feeling pretty good. Your minimizing muscles are getting stronger and you've already tackled three key spaces in your home. You started with your own stuff—your clothing and personal products—and have slowly spread out to begin having an influence on more shared areas, like the kitchen.

Your little pebble is making some serious ripples in the pond, and your family should be standing up and taking notice. If you're minimizing while respecting their space, you should be getting some curious questions and even some assistance! That's great! I could spend the rest of this book taking you room-by-room through the rest of your house, but you know what? You don't need that. You understand how to use the LESS Method™ to systematically minimize the excess stuff in your life.

Like I said, the way I tackle a closet is the same way I tackle a basement and the same way I tackle a garage. The method doesn't change. The space does. So, map out a plan of where you want to go next (or just let your instinct lead the way) and go for it!

What's that I hear? I believe you said, "Yeah, but ... " As you should. Sure, the LESS Method™ works in a garage or a basement, but what about paper? And all that memorabilia you said to set aside? And how do I deal with the holidays?

The next three chapters are devoted to some of these tricky areas and special situations that often crop up when we embark on a minimalism mission. I'm here to answer your "Yeah, buts … " with some tried-and-true advice that will hopefully keep you from getting stuck in some common minimizing roadblocks.

Let's start with paper.

Paper is a beast. It's one of the trickiest areas to control because it never stops coming into your house. Sure, you can stop buying shoes and trinkets, but unless you want to superglue your mailbox shut or refuse to allow your children to bring their backpacks home from school, you can't stop paper from coming into your life on a nearly daily basis. I always tell clients, "You will never feel organized until you have your paper under control." If you don't have a game plan for attacking paper, it won't be long before you've got a paper-tastic clutter fest going on 24/7.

Deny, Deny, Deny

The first step to controlling your paper is to do what every organized crime boss's lawyer tells him to do and *Deny, Deny, Deny*. When offered unnecessary paper at work conferences, school open houses, or your bank, politely refuse it. "No thanks, I'll just check out your website" is a perfectly fine response to a person who wants to hand you a pamphlet detailing all their services or products. Get used to saying "No thanks" a lot.

But sometimes you need a more offensive strategy to paper prevention and this is where the Internet is your friend. Here are three websites and an app (all current at time of printing) that will help stop junk mail from coming to your house:

- **Catalogchoice.org** – Allows you to select specific catalogs you'd like to stop receiving.

- **Dmachoice.org** – For a small fee ($2 at time of printing) this site will unsubscribe you from all unsolicited promotional mail.

- **Optoutprescreen.com** - Prevents you from receiving credit and insurance offers. You can choose to be removed from these lists for five years or you can print and mail a signed form to be removed permanently.

- **Paper Karma** – An app that allows you to snap pictures of company logos and return addresses on unwanted junk mail in order to unsubscribe.

If you really want to get serious about denying paper access to your home, do all of the above. And do it for your spouse, too. If visiting three websites and downloading one app seems like too much work, I must ask ... how much work are you doing clearing paper piles off your countertops every time you want eat a meal?

The Giant Inbox

Yes, you can take a hard line toward stopping paper from coming into your house, but what about the paper that is already there? If you have paper piles covering your countertops like little mounds of 8 ½ x 11 snow, you need to address them.

The first step is scary, but it's similar to what we did using the LESS Method™ in the other areas of your house: get it all together. Grab as many laundry baskets, cardboard boxes, and other containment receptacles as you need and gather all your loose paper into a centralized location. I call this the "giant inbox" and yes, right now it will look huge and scary. When I do this with clients, we often have four or five giant inboxes when we start. That's normal. It will not always be this way, but to attack your paper issue, you must understand the totality of what you're dealing with.

Think about the difference between traditional and guerrilla warfare. It's much easier to address your enemy in the light of day than to ferret them out of the jungle. Get your paper out in the open. Don't let it hide in your corners, closets, and drawers, ready to ambush you when you least expect it.

The RAFT System

You've got your paper all together in a giant inbox and you're staring at that enemy across the field. Your palms are starting to sweat. There are just so many of them! And only one of you. How can you possibly win?

I hear you. And I've got a solution: RAFT. If you're drowning in paper, a RAFT is a life-saver (pun fully intended). This acronym is often used by professional organizers to help clients manage paper. You can use RAFT to make sense of your giant inbox by sorting it into four different piles:

Read

Action

File

Trash

Let's talk about each of those a wee bit.

Read: This is all the paper, such as magazines or catalogues, that you plan to read at some point in the near future. Put all your "To Read" items in a bin or basket near your couch or bed, wherever you do your reading. And let's keep it real. Are you really going to read 15 magazines and 20 catalogues? Keep your To Read basket current and reasonable. And when next month's magazine issue arrives, let last month's go. Yes, even if you didn't read it. And hey, if you didn't read it, do you really need that magazine subscription, anyway?

Action: These are all the papers that require you to do something (pay a bill, sign a permission slip, call your insurance agent, etc.) Put all your actionable paper into an "Action Basket" somewhere conspicuous, like a kitchen counter. Work from this basket on a daily basis to get yo' stuff done.

File: This is the paper that you want to save for reference by putting it into a filing system. Think tax info, insurance policies, medical records, car maintenance history, etc. To keep your filing from just becoming a more organized version of paper clutter, I recommend you ask yourself three questions before committing paper to your files:

1) **Is it RELEVANT?** For example, if it's car insurance information, is it for your current car with your current company? If it's a bill, has it been paid without dispute from either side? If so, do you still need it?

2) **Is it the MOST RECENT?** Do you get a statement like this every month or every six months? Is this the most current one you have? (You don't need any others, my friend.)

3) **Can I find it ELSEWHERE?** This is a biggie. Do you get an email every month with this same info? Do you have an account with online access? Could you make one phone call and have this same information? If so, then drop that paper like a bad habit! You don't need to spend your precious time filing something to which you have alternate access.

Trash: Or Recycle or Shred. I'm an environmentally friendly gal, and I also don't want you flapping your private info out there like Marilyn Monroe over a subway grate. Recycle what you can, shred what you should, and think about how happy you will be to have all this excess paper out of your life!

But I Hate Filing!

Of course you do. You and everybody else who's ever filed something. Nobody loves to file stuff but everybody likes being able to find their stuff. (Note: The IRS likes that, too.) And filing is the best way I've found to be able to retrieve important information when you need it.

Can't I Just Scan Everything Instead?

Sure! If you prefer to scan and keep your files digitally, go for it. I got no beef with that. Interestingly, people often ask me if I'm 100% paperless. They assume because I'm a minimalist that I must have no paper in my house. But my dirty little secret is, I actually like having paper copies of some things. (Major scandal, I know.)

Like most people, I'm a hybrid of paper and digital storage. I think this comes from being a Gen X-er or Gen Y-er or Millennial or whatever the heck they call people who came of age as the Internet was born. I typed my third-grade book report on a typewriter, but I made websites in college. So, I keep some information digitally and some things on paper. No big deal. Do what works for you, but the most important thing is, *do something*. Don't let paper rule your life. Take charge and be able to find your important info when you need it.

Keep Those Files Close

One trick to making filing a lot easier? Keep your files nearby. And when I say nearby, I mean fingertip distance from wherever you sort your paper. Typically, this is somewhere near the kitchen. (Remember, it's the heart of the home. Everything happens in the kitchen!)

If a filing cabinet in your kitchen isn't your style, you can purchase a mobile filing cart that can be rolled into your pantry or a nearby closet when not in use. Filing fails when it is tucked away in the basement or an office on the second floor. Nobody, not even me, will walk up a flight of stairs or down a long hallway to file a piece of paper.

In fact, my files are within three feet of me right now as I type. And I'm typing at my dining room table where my children just ate oatmeal and are now fighting over a pillow pet. But hey, if you wanted to know my car insurance deductible, I could find it for you in one-minute flat. I call that winning.

Eat that Elephant

RAFT will help you dwindle that giant inbox down to zero, but it might not happen overnight, depending on how big your inbox is. Set realistic goals for how much paper you can handle sorting at a time. Thirty minutes? An hour? Remember that famous advice for how to eat an elephant—one bite at a time. (Although why someone would want to eat an elephant, I have no idea. I'd prefer if this analogy involved a 12-foot long sub sandwich or a swimming pool-sized bowl of spaghetti.)

If paper has been a problem for years, it will take a while to clear your backlog. Don't let that discourage you. Keep eating that elephant/massive sub/spaghetti pool, one small bite—or 30-minute session—at a time and it will get done.

If it helps, turn on some tunes, have mindless TV going in the background, wear a silly hat, whatever motivates you to keep going. When I tackled my paper piles originally, I drank wine during the process. It definitely helped make a tedious process more enjoyable. And I even started to giggle as I read my backlog of car insurance info. I have a preferred rate?? Sweeeeeeet!!! I think we could all raise a glass to being paper clutter free.

Maintain Your Gain, er, Loss

It would be so awesome if you did all of the above and your paper problems stayed gone forever, right? But like all spaces in your house, you will need to practice a few simple habits to keep your paper piles from coming back.

- **Deny, deny, deny!** Practice your paper refusal skills on a daily basis and you will soon feel like a pro.

- **Use RAFT Every Day:** Get in the habit of giving your paper the RAFT treatment on a daily basis, as soon as it comes in the door. You'll get so good at this that paper will start to fear your ninja skills!

- **Follow the One In/One Out Rule:** When you file a piece of paper, pull an old one to shred or recycle. This is what I always do with insurance statements. I am sent a new one every six months, so I file that one and shred the old one.

- **Keep Extra Filing Supplies Handy:** Your life is going to change so you are going to need to make new files at some point. You'll have a baby, buy a car, or need surgery and suddenly you have new paper that doesn't fit into your old categories. DO NOT LET LIFE CHANGES DERAIL YOUR FILING SYSTEM! All you need to do is make a new file and add it to the existing ones. However, I find that this is where filing breaks down for most people. They don't make the new file, so the new paper builds up, the old paper gets older, and voila! Welcome back, paper piles! To combat this, *never fill your filing drawers more than ¾ full.* Nothing discourages your filing efforts more than trying to cram a folder into an already stuffed drawer. Use that back quarter to house extra folders, so when you need to make a new file, just grab a pen and bam! It's done! No searching around your house for supplies or piling that paper on top of the cabinet because it's too much work to file it. Make filing so easy that it seems ridiculous NOT to do it. Then you can move on to the more important work of living your life.

- **Have an Annual Shred Party:** Aw, yeah! Nothing says party time like a Hawaiian shirt and a shredder going full blast! Silly as it sounds, hosting an annual shred party with your files will help you purge ones that are no longer necessary. If you work in an office, see if you can get your boss to buy in on this. I'm thinking casual Friday, snacks, tunes, and a big ol' stack of shreddables. Ah, workplace productivity at its finest!

To Review

If you wanna get your paper under control, follow these steps:

1. **Giant inbox:** Gather together all your loose paper into one area.

2. **RAFT:** Sort your inbox into Read, Action, File, and Trash.

3. **Maintain:**

    a. Deny, Deny, Deny

    b. RAFT

    c. One In/One Out for filing

    d. Keep filing supplies nearby

    e. Annual shred party

CHAPTER 12

Yeah, But ... What About Memorabilia?

You knew we'd get here, right? You've been setting aside memorabilia from all different parts of your house and now you are ready to deal with it. By the way, if you are reading this chapter and you have NOT minimized the rest of your house and set aside memorabilia, go back and do that. Trust me on this: you want to deal with memorabilia last, as a category unto itself, only after you have minimized pretty much every other space.

Why? Because this stuff can be really, really emotional. You will find surprising things that will make you react in ways you can't anticipate. I helped my mom downsize a few years ago and we started in her storage room. (Bad idea, by the way. We should have started somewhere easier.)

One of the first things we came across was a picture of her at two years old, sitting on Santa's knee. She said she didn't want to keep the picture, but as soon she put it in the trash, she started to cry. So I started to cry. So then we were both hugging and crying and not really minimizing anything. Not an effective way to start the whole downsizing process.

Trust me, you don't want to take this on if you haven't built up some minimizing muscle from other parts of your house. If you've got some decluttering practice under your belt, you will be mentally ready to tackle your memorabilia and, unlike me and my mom, hopefully avoid profuse crying at pictures of kids on Santa's lap.

Definition & Mantra

Let's start by setting a clear definition of memorabilia. I consider memorabilia: *anything kept for the purpose of memory rather than for use or display.* That said, I strongly encourage you to use and display your memorabilia. I have a lovely wall tapestry that Josh and I got on our honeymoon in Nepal. It is displayed proudly over our couch, and every time I yell at my kids to stop pulling on it, I pause for a second to think fondly of our time in Nepal, before kids, when we could sleep in and drink tea on a rooftop overlooking the Himalayas. When we felt like we were more in love than anyone else had ever been in love, and that we were really *living life*, we had it all figured out, and a wall tapestry was just a wall tapestry, safely secured on a wall where it belongs, in no danger of sudden removal by sticky maple-syrup hands. *Sigh.*

Where was I? Oh yeah, memorabilia.

For most people, including me, it is not feasible to use or display all your memorabilia. I think it's fine to keep some things just for the sake of memory. I have one tub of personal memorabilia in the attic that contains items such as:

- A book of poetry I wrote in high school. No one understood my pain. *No one.* And this book is proof of that.

- My baby book, containing a lock of my baby-fine hair. I don't know why, but of everything else my mom put in this book, the hair is my favorite part.

- A story I wrote in 6th grade called *The Personal Diary of Sophia Sock.* It is—you guessed it—a story about the adventures of a sock. I think future historians will find this and realize I was way ahead of my time.

- A big clear envelope labeled "The Mommy Years" where I put all my favorite drawings and homemade cards from my kiddos.

One mantra I've adopted as I've sorted my own memorabilia and helped others sort theirs is: *only two things can happen to memorabilia over time—it can become more important or it can become less important.* I urge you to keep this in mind as you tackle those tubs. Just because you saved something once (or perhaps, your Great Aunt Sally saved something once) does not mean you need to save it forever.

For example, I used to save every single birthday and anniversary card I received. These cards seemed important to me at the time. But when I minimized my memorabilia, I realized that most of these cards had lost their importance over time. So I let them go, keeping only the few that had grown in importance over the years.

How will you know whether something has increased or decreased in importance? Just follow the advice of the Swedish pop rock duo Roxette in their 1988 hit song "Listen to Your Heart" and just, well, listen to your heart. When it's calling for you. Listen to your heart. There's nothing else you can do. (I think I've pretty much covered the message of the entire song now.)

4 Key Questions to Help You Sort Memorabilia

With your definition and mantra in mind—and Roxette's "Listen to Your Heart" perhaps playing in the background—gather all your memorabilia into one place. This should be pretty easy since you've been setting it aside as you decluttered your other rooms. Drag out all the boxes, tubs, and bins into the light of day. It's time to make some decisions, and the best way to do that is to ask yourself four key questions.

Question 1: How Much Do I Want to Keep?

Asking yourself how much you want to keep will set clear limits for the amount of memorabilia you allow into your life. For whatever reason, I always quantify memorabilia in terms of tubs. How many tubs do you want to dedicate to memorabilia? One? Ten? None? The number really doesn't matter, as long as you have the space and are okay with maintaining it.

Personally, I keep one tub of memorabilia for myself and one for each of the kids. Josh, on the other hand, probably has four or five. He likes to keep more memorabilia than me, and that's okay.

I had one client who followed my process and set aside all her memorabilia as we decluttered her house. When we got to the last step of deciding on memorabilia she said, "I've thought about this a lot and I'm going to keep all of it. Memorabilia is the one thing that brings me the most joy." That's cool. She is the type of person who truly enjoys looking through memorabilia when she has spare time. She has space for it in her house, and she is dedicated to maintaining it. She should keep all her memorabilia.

I am not that type of person. I used to have eight tubs of memorabilia and it made me feel crazy. My one tub is just enough for me. Your memorabilia tub limit is very personal, but I urge you—*set a limit*. Otherwise memorabilia can very quickly overwhelm your space and you won't be able to actually enjoy it.

Question 2: *How* Do I Want to Keep It?

Another way to phrase this question is, "In what form do I want to keep it?" I'm not a scrap booker. Not at all. Not even a little bit. I will take this moment to apologize to my crafty daughter Mercedes for this. I don't understand those scissors that cut different types of curly lines. What's wrong with the straight line? Anyway, I know that the only form in which I will keep memorabilia is the original form.

If it's a T-shirt, it stays a T-shirt; if it's a trophy, it stays a trophy; if it's a certificate of achievement from a 3rd grade spelling bee, it stays what it is. I will not shrink, cut, or in any other way modify my memorabilia. I am happy for those who do these things, but this is a thing I cannot do.

For me, this makes deciding on memorabilia easier, because it keeps me from turning my memorabilia into a project. Often, clients tell me they want to use their memorabilia to create a scrapbook. That's great! But *a scrapbook is a project,* a dedication of your time, and judging by the many different kinds of crafty scissors out there, a lot of your time.

If you truly enjoy scrapbooking and want to take on the project of scrapbooking all your memorabilia, go for it. But if you don't want to do that, don't. It's okay to just keep memorabilia as it is or let it go or hire someone to make a scrapbook for you. Google it. These people exist.

If you don't have enough space to keep your memorabilia as it is and you don't want to scrapbook, here are a few other ways to manage memorabilia:

Digitize it: This is my favorite way to deal with memorabilia. Taking pictures is a way to preserve your memories and be able to enjoy them for years to come. Digitizing is especially great for clunky memorabilia, like furniture, trophies and wedding dresses. I remember the day I donated my wedding dress. I paused before putting it on my donation pile, but then I asked myself, "Do I have a picture of me in this dress?" Yes, of course! And I look great—young, tan, happy. That's how I want to remember this dress, not as a dusty relic in my closet.

So, I put it happily on the pile of donations, and have never regretted it. Not even when I saw it for sale in the Halloween section at Goodwill a few weeks later. (True story!) I laughed out loud. Somebody was going to be a zombie bride in my wedding dress! Judge me if you will, but I thought that was a great way to repurpose an item that marked such a happy day in my life. It brought me much joy, and now it will bring joy, of a different sort, to someone else. And maybe first prize in a costume contest, as well. Who knows?

Make a quilt: If you have a lot of fabric memorabilia—like T-shirts, communion gowns, and curtains from your baby's nursery—a quilt is an excellent way to keep a small piece of each of these memories. And my favorite part of creating a quilt is that you can use it! Not a quilter? Again, let me introduce you to my friend Google. Go find someone who is.

Keep one piece: If you have a large collection of something, try keeping just one piece. For example, if you have an entire set of china dishes, you could keep just one serving platter to use for special occasions. This is a much better way to enjoy that china than letting it sit in a dusty box in your attic.

Share it: I have found that the hardest memorabilia for me to part with is my kids' artwork. I digitize a lot of it, but another great solution I've found is mailing it to out-of-town grandmas, off-at-college babysitters, and childless aunts and uncles. You could even drop artwork off at a nursing home to brighten the day of lonely residents. Share the love!

One caveat: don't use the share option to simply dump your unwanted memorabilia off on others. Before you decide to share memorabilia, really think about whether or not this memorabilia would add value to the life of someone else. And—this one's a biggie—don't give it with guilt or the expectation that the other person should keep it forever. That's not a gift, that's an obligation. When you give a gift, it belongs to someone else and they get to decide what to do with it. If you can't give in this way, you shouldn't give at all.

Question 3: How does this make me feel?

Remember my memorabilia mantra? *Only two things can happen to memorabilia over time—it can become more important or it can become less important.* This is where you really need to listen to your gut.

You will have an immediate emotional reaction to your memorabilia. Believe me, I see this on client's faces every day when they discover all their math worksheets from 4th grade or the crib bumpers from their now high school child's nursery or the collection of jewelry boxes from their grandmother. I can tell which items they no longer care about, which items make them feel happy, and which items make them feel bad. And oddly, we often keep a lot of memorabilia that makes us feel bad.

When I sorted my photographs from childhood, I found quite a few pictures of my Grandpa Orlando. He died when I was in high school and the pictures of him in his later years show the signs of his slow decline into dementia and Alzheimer's. Looking at these pictures made me feel sad. I remembered the pain of watching my strong build-the-roof-yourself grandfather decline into a skinny shell of his former self. I remembered the lost, frightened look in his eyes. Even writing this makes me tear up.

So, I decided I didn't want those pictures. None of them. I threw them all away.

Again, judge me if you will, but I kept all the pictures of him young and healthy: sitting in his favorite chair with a small me on his lap, sucking my thumb; outside at our house in Michigan, dressed in his work clothes, helping my dad install a new septic system; standing next to his pride and joy—his beautiful garden—where he grew the most delicious tomatoes you've ever eaten.

These are the memories I want of my grandfather; these are the pictures I kept. Now, when I look through my photo album from childhood, I can see my grandfather the way I want to remember him: healthy, strong, and full of life.

Also, be very aware of any memorabilia you might be saving out of guilt. I once helped a client sort her basement and we came across a framed cross-stitching her grandmother had made. I could tell by her face that this object stirred some negative feelings, but she immediately said, "I have to keep that." So, I set it aside in her memorabilia area until the end of our session. As we were cleaning up, I pointed to the picture again and said, "So you are keeping that, right?"

She sighed. "I guess so."

I laughed. "That doesn't sound very convincing!"

"When we were cleaning out my grandma's apartment, I was going to donate that, but my grandma's neighbor saw it in the hallway and said, 'You can't get rid of that!' So I kept it."

We talked through why it was okay for her to let this go, that she did not have to hang on to this picture to honor her grandmother, and especially not to honor the wishes of a nosy neighbor. She donated the picture that day, and I imagine it is now happily hanging in the home of someone who truly enjoys it.

As you sort your memorabilia, listen to that little voice inside you. It will tell you if these items are still important. You may have outgrown them or feel indifferent toward them. They may make you feel happy or they may actually make you feel bad. Free yourself from memorabilia you are keeping out of guilt, fear, or a sense of obligation. We are all the keepers of our own memories, so we get to decide which memories we want to keep. And doesn't it make sense to only keep memories that make us feel truly happy?

Question 4: Who Am I Saving This For?

A really good English teacher would reword that subheading, "For whom am I saving this?" And since I know a lot of really good English teachers, feel free to get out the red pen and correct. But for the rest of you who don't give two craps about ending sentences with prepositions, let's cut the grammar and focus in:

Who are you saving this for?

This is a big one. When I whittled my eight boxes of memorabilia down to one, this was the question that helped me do it. I prefer to reword the question this way: *Who really wants to look at this stuff?* I asked myself this question repeatedly as I dug through my eight tubs, and here were my answers:

My kids? Probably not. They might browse through a few photos of me in a high school yearbook, but they'll never pore over every certificate of achievement I received in my illustrious academic career.

Me? Highly doubtful. I hadn't looked at most of that stuff since the day I (or my mom—love you, Mom!) tossed it in the tubs. What made me think I'd suddenly want to spend an afternoon browsing through every article I wrote for my college newspaper?

My mom? Heck, no! As soon as I had my own house, she dropped those boxes off on my porch like a baby on the orphanage steps! She clearly didn't want any of it.

As awesome as I am, I had to face the #1 memorabilia fact: *no one really cares much about it.* To soften the blow of fact #1, consider fact #2: *That's totally okay.*

Let me explain. You are living in the present. Your memorabilia is your past. And as hard as it sometimes is to admit, the past is gone. Memorabilia is our weak human attempt to do something impossible: save time. So instead of spending hours looking through scrapbooks from long-forgotten trips, take yourself out for ice cream, call a friend, read a book. Do something, and do it now, because now is all you have. Carpe diem!

Secondly, this stuff is not you. It is not your family. It is not your friends. I am not my Brownie sash, nor am I my varsity letter. Those are just things. Memories live in your heart and your mind, not in your stuff.

Finally, you are you, with or without the stuff. I am still smart and insightful, even though I no longer have every A paper I wrote for senior English. I still love to travel, even though I no longer have that half-finished scrapbook from a high school trip to Europe. I still love my family and friends, even though I no longer have every birthday card those wonderful folks sent me.

Ask yourself, *who am I saving this for?* And listen carefully to your answer. It is there, inside you, and it will tell you what you should do.

Why You Shouldn't Save Memorabilia for Your Kids

I would be remiss if I did not take a moment to address my fellow tender-hearted mamas and papas out there and discuss the issue of saving memorabilia for your kids. This is a tricky issue, and one that I've dealt with in different ways as my kids have grown.

I won't claim to have it 100% figured out, but I will stand behind the subheading of this section and tell you straight: You shouldn't save memorabilia for your kids. Let me explain.

In almost every class I teach, someone asks this question: "A few years ago, my mom dropped off like 10 boxes of stuff from my childhood. What do I do with it?"

This is very common. Parents—because they love their children in that sense-defying way all parents love their children—save stuff from their kids' childhoods. Eventually the parents, unsure of what to do with the items they've saved, pass them off to their grown children, usually to glowing receptions like, "Um, yeah ... thanks, Mom ... "

Because here's the deal: the memories in those boxes don't belong to the child. They belong to the parent. Which is why one of my organizing mantras is: *the only person you should only save memorabilia for is yourself.*

Easier said than done, as I learned recently.

Backtrack about five years: I buy each of my kids one see-through plastic tub to use for memorabilia. I think to myself, "Ah-ha! I'm ahead of the game! I'll never be that mom who drops off the unwanted tubs 'o stuff on her grown children's porches! I've soooooo got this!" I resolve to limit each kid to one tub, which they can take with them when they (sniff) eventually move out.

I start putting things in the tubs: their baby bracelets from the hospital, the tee-tiny knitted hats they wore in the NICU, the orange plastic spoon my son Orlando carried 24/7 for two years of his toddlerhood.

Fast forward to last spring: My son Reese kills it at his Cub Scout Pinewood Derby, taking home a trophy, a medal, and several patches. (Those Boy Scouts are really, really into the patches. It's like a thing.) I realize he is a champion of racing a little wooden car proudly made by his father and that perhaps he needs a place to store his growing collection of memorabilia. Enter the tubs. I head up to the attic, where I had been keeping them, and prepare to officially bequeath the plastic memory holders to my children.

However, before bringing the tubs down, I spend a few moments reminiscing about the items already inside. The NICU lovies that still smell like the hospital, the locks of hair from their first haircuts.

I start to feel a little odd about giving these items to my children, and I'm not sure why. I ask myself, "If my kids wanted to get rid of these things, how would I feel?" Immediately, my heart lurches in a million different devastating directions. There is *no way* I can allow my kids to part with these memories, because … it slowly dawns on me … these are *my* memories, not theirs.

They don't remember the NICU. They don't remember their first haircuts or what they wore home from the hospital. But I do. I need to save these memories for myself, not burden my children with "memory" items of which they have absolutely no recollection.

Somewhere in the back of my head, I hear my own voice at one of my organizing classes: *the only person you should save memorabilia for is yourself.*

Touché.

So, I removed the baby items and put them in my own memorabilia tub, where my kids and I can both look at them if we want to. I will let my kids forge their own memories, saving whatever memorabilia matters to them.

I give them their tubs, and we talk about what "memorabilia" means, how it is different from toys. I explain that it's something you keep because it reminds you of a special time. We also talk about what happens if the memorabilia tub gets full.

"We have to take something out," they respond immediately. (Wow, these kids must have a professional organizer mom!)

So my daughter puts in a postcard her Uncle Jake sent her from his tour of duty in Afghanistan. Reese puts in a ceramic lizard he painted in Mexico. Orlando adds a drawing his brother made him last week.

I smile. They've got this. They are keeping their memories, and I am keeping mine. And that's the way it should be.

Mamas and papas, let's do our kids a favor and allow them to keep the memories that matter to them, while we keep those that matter to us. I think we'll all be happier in the end, and this will save us a tub-dropping drive-by at our adult kids' houses one day. Hoorah!

CHAPTER 13

Yeah, But ... What About Gifts?

Gifts can cause a real conundrum for minimalists and those who love them. What do you give someone who doesn't want a lot of stuff? How do you celebrate holidays, especially with little kids, without focusing on gifts? And what do you do when well-intended loved ones give you things you don't want?

These are valid—and difficult—questions. I don't claim to have all the answers, but I've learned a few things about gift-giving on this minimalism journey that might be helpful to you. And believe me, I'm still learning!

Relationships Before Principles

If you desire a minimalist lifestyle and you have a history of centering holidays and birthdays around gifts, you will need to turn the gift train around. And believe me, the wheels will squeak. Loudly. Changing how you give and receive gifts might surprise/shock/anger your loved ones, so to avoid some negative backlash, it's very important that you talk about it. Up front. A lot.

Communication is key, and remember: just because you send the message doesn't mean the other person receives it. That's not their fault. People have probably sent you many messages in your life that you misinterpreted. In fact, the entire message of this book has been that Jon Bon Jovi is the sexiest man alive. Wait, you didn't get that? It's Chapter 13, for Pete's sake!

So be patient with others—and yourself. You are doing something new.

When talking to family and friends about gifts, my goal is to open conversations, not change them. Call me crazy, but people don't really respond well when you try to change them. If Grandma likes to buy your kids lots of presents, try opening a conversation with her, something like, "We're experimenting with giving the kids different kinds of gifts this year. What would you think about getting them a museum pass or a dance class?"

Now Grandma may very well say, "No, thank you" and continue on with business as usual. That's her right. But you should still pat yourself on the back. You opened the conversation! And now that it's open, guess what? You can go back to it whenever you want! It's as simple as, "Remember when I talked about getting Johnny that museum pass? He'd still really like that and his birthday is coming up. Here's a link to the museum website, if you're interested." Again, opening, not trying to change. Not saying, "Stop buying all that crap for my kids!" even though I know that's what you want to say.

My wise minimalist friend Jenna once gave me this mantra: *Relationships before principles.* Sure, we might be minimalists and feel like we don't need stuff, and that's great. But our relationships with the people who love us are much more important than that. Rejecting their gifts—which are often symbols of their love—is a surefire way to damage the relationship.

Open those conversations, slowly but surely, with plenty of love and room for the other person to have a say, and you might be surprised that the gift train wheel gets a little less squeaky over time.

I hope the next two sections will give you some food-for-thought when it comes to receiving and giving gifts, minimalist style.

Receiving Gifts: Keep the Love, Not the Stuff

Every time I sort a space with a client, we find at least one: a guilty gift.

Guilty gifts are usually given to us by some wonderful person whom we love dearly. The only problem is ... we don't love the gift. It's not our color or our style. We may not even be sure what it is exactly. Yet we keep it, because we love the giver, and also because the thought of letting it go makes us feel very, very guilty.

But I'm here to tell you: *you can keep the love without keeping the stuff.*

I think of gifts as vehicles for love and goodwill. Let's say that my boss gives me a mug with the company logo. I love the company, I may even love my boss, but that does not mean I love this mug. She gave me the mug as a symbol of her goodwill, basically saying, "I think you're great and I'm glad you work here." (And also, let's be honest, "We got a better deal on these mugs if we bought 500 of them, so here you go! Coffee break starts in 5 minutes!")

But instead of telling me these words, she let the mug do the talking. I receive the mug, I receive the love. After that? I say a sincere, "Thank you." After all, she gave me love and goodwill, and I am always thankful for that! And then I'm free to do with that mug as I will. I can find it a new home, I can repurpose it, I can even sell it, if I so choose. The point is: *I get to keep the love, which is the most valuable part of the gift.*

I know this may make you nervous, especially when you consider sentimental gifts, those received from loved ones, particularly loved ones who have passed on. Naturally, these gifts give us more pause than the company mug. But the basic principle is the same.

Your loved ones are saying, "I love you. You are important to me." And instead of actually saying that, they're letting Grandma's china do the talking. Again, we can choose to think of Grandma's china as a vehicle for her love. Keep the love, revel in it, but find the china a new home if you don't love it, too.

Because here's what happens if you don't: *you negate some of the love by allowing your guilty feelings to cloud it.* If you don't love Grandma's china, every time you look at it, your internal dialogue goes something like: "Oh man ... Grandma gave me that china and I never use it. I feel so bad ... I'm a bad granddaughter. I don't know what to do ... Ugh. I just want to close this cupboard and not think about it."

You don't need a psychologist to tell you that these are very NEGATIVE feelings. No one wants to feel like that, and Grandma definitely does *not* want you to feel like that. Because while you're sweating guilt about her plates, you know what you're *not* doing? Thinking of her with love. That's what she wants. Your guilt is clouding the true, loving feelings you have for her.

Snap a pic of that china, or save a special piece that you can actually use, and then let it go, knowing that you are enabling yourself to honor your grandmother's memory more fondly by NOT keeping all her china.

Remember: *you can keep the love without keeping the stuff.*

Does this principle apply to gifts we give, too? Absolutely. I expect to be thanked for gifts. After all, the gift is a vehicle for my *love!* Say thank you! But after that, I realize it's up to the recipient whether or not the actual item suits her life. I've watched my kids donate gifts from me. I've even helped friends donate gifts from me, which I've found in their closets when I helped them declutter. Ha! I don't ever feel bad about this. The gift is not me; it's just a thing. I know they love me even if they can't use the gift I gave them.

If you have guilty gifts in your life, could you remove some negativity by finding those gifts a new home? I give you full permission to *keep all that love* … and let the stuff go.

Giving Gifts: The Easter Basket Conundrum

I remember one of my first Easters after adopting minimalism. I was teaching full-time and had waited until the Thursday before Easter to think about the contents of my kids' Easter baskets. Thus, I found myself at my local superstore, surrounded by what I will refer to as "plastic crap." You know the stuff: wind-up bunny toys, teensy portions of modeling clay encased in plastic eggs, and bin after bin of stuffed bunnies and chicks.

My kids didn't need any of this stuff. I felt suckered. Was this what Easter was reduced to? An aisle of cheaply made trinkets that most kids would toss within a few hours? I felt frustrated, and worse yet, I had no alternative, given my holiday procrastination.

I made the best of the situation, selecting items my kids could use, such as sidewalk chalk and bath toys. I also guiltily added ample amounts of candy, because I knew candy wouldn't end up in the trash.

In the end, I caved a bit and bought Matchbox cars for my boys and a stuffed animal (yes, a stuffed animal ... the worst of the clutter-causing toys!) for Mercedes. I paid for my overpriced tchotchkes, knowing I'd learned a valuable lesson: to be a minimalist in a consumer culture, one must plan for the holidays.

This lesson was further driven home when my kids opened their baskets on Easter morning. They immediately stuffed as much candy as possible into their little cheeks before I put the kibosh on their sugar gorge. As for the plastic crap? They ignored it completely.

The lesson-learning continued later that day, when I set about the task of incorporating the new stuff into our existing toy collection. Using the One In/One Out rule, I carefully selected two old Matchbox cars and replaced them with the two new. I then removed one old stuffed animal and replaced it with the one new. (Note: this was before I learned to involve my kids in the donating process.)

Even I felt the futility of this gesture. To simply replace like with like, isn't this the problem in our culture? We simply cannot stand to keep our perfectly usable older things. We are enticed by "new" things that aren't really all that different from what we already have. Isn't this why landfills are overflowing? Ah, the best lessons in life are learned the hard way, are they not?

I had been schooled by the Easter Bunny. And I resolved to not let the Easter Basket Conundrum repeat itself at the next holiday. I set 10 guidelines for myself when purchasing gifts. Perhaps they will help you, too.

Rose's Top Ten Gift-Giving Guidelines

1. **Buy Something They Need.** Most kids do not need toys of the plastic crap variety. What they do need, however, are pajamas, clean toothbrushes, socks, and hairbrushes. If your kids need these things,

buy them; heck, even buy them plastered with pictures of their favorite superheroes.

2. **Go Big.** My wise sister-in-law, Gabby, taught me this lesson. For Easter, she buys her kids one large item instead of a basket full of small ones. One year she bought her son Jonas a new pogo stick to replace his broken one, her daughter Willah a pair of roller skates, and her youngest, Lizzy, her first big-girl bike.

3. **Develop a Motto.** A teaching colleague of mine introduced me to this gift-buying motto: *Something you want, something you need, something to wear, and something to read.* Following this motto really checks the impulse to over-buy. Even if I found myself stuck in a superstore the Thursday before a holiday, I could follow it to buy simple, basic gifts for my family. And imagine if you taught your kids this motto early on! They would know exactly what to expect when birthdays and holidays rolled around.

   My family has adopted a "One Big, Two Small" policy. I've also heard this called the Three Wise Men rule (i.e. three wise men = three gifts). For birthdays and Christmas, my kids make two wish lists: one for big items and one for small. They know they will get one item from their big list and two items from their small list.

   The definitions of "big" and "small" are up to them. For example, one year Reese asked for an electric scooter on his big list, while Orlando asked for a blanket with his favorite cartoon character. The price discrepancy between these gifts was huge, but both boys were happy because they got what they considered to be big gifts.

   Whatever rule or motto you set is fine, but I think it's important to set one. Your family will come to accept this as the norm, and it will dramatically decrease the amount of clutter entering your life.

4. **Recycle.** Gabby and I made a pact one Christmas: instead of buying new gifts, her kids each chose a toy they no longer played with to give to my kids, their younger cousins. I still remember Gabby telling me how Lizzy spent hours washing and brushing her My Little Ponies to give to Mercedes. How sweet! Recycling toys is an easy, economical

way for kids to give each other meaningful gifts. It's also good for the environment. Score!

5. **Go Martha.** By this I mean channel your inner Martha Stewart and make something yourself. Every Christmas my neighbor Kevin brings us a plate of homemade cookies. I always look forward to this gift, and it doesn't feel like Christmas until I see Kevin on my porch, cookies in hand. When I taught middle school, I spent the weeks before winter break helping my students craft gifts of writing to their loved ones. My students always came back in January, eager to tell of the teary-eyed hugs and thank you's they received for these gifts.

You have some sort of talent: woodworking, knitting, painting, writing. Use it to create meaningful gifts. Do what you do best, and your loved ones will feel the love.

6. **Buy Consumables.** This might sound like it goes against everything I just said, but stay put. Sometimes you simply have to buy something, right? You can't knit scarves for your entire office and giving a set of homemade coasters to your boss might seem a bit inappropriate. By consumable, I mean things that can be used without creating a lot of waste.

For kids, think paints, crayons, bubbles, or sidewalk chalk. For adults, think wine, fancy chocolates, lotion, and candles. Be warned, though: if you give an adult all four of those items at once, they may think you're trying to seduce them. So maybe stick with just one, unless of course, you are trying to seduce them, in which case, buy them all and good luck!

7. **Give Experiences.** Museum memberships, pottery classes, a night at a bed-and-breakfast, massages, manicures, etc. You get the idea. Experience gifts are wonderful because the memories made can last a lifetime.

8. **Give Gift Cards or Cash.** Yeah, yeah, I know some people say gift cards and cash aren't thoughtful or they're not real gifts. But I've rarely received a gift card I haven't used and seriously, who doesn't want cash? One year my parents moved right before the holidays and

my mom didn't have time to go shopping, so she gave all of us crisp bills folded to look like stars and Christmas trees. There were no fake "thank you's" under the tree that year!

9. **Give to a Cause.** What charitable causes do your loved ones care about? Rescuing abused animals? Building schools in third world countries? Stopping rainforest destruction? Charitable donations not only support worthy causes, but they also show that you thought about the specific heartstrings of the receiver. Nice!

10. **Give Your Time.** During one of my minimalism classes last fall, a woman said her 13-year-old grandson asked her for only one birthday gift: a day for just him and her. I can still hear the spontaneous "Awww!" from the group when she shared that.

I think we underestimate the gift of our time. I doubt anyone gets to the end of their life and thinks, "Man! I'm really glad my sister gave me that set of mini-cupcake pans in '05. What a difference it has made in my life!" I would imagine, rather, that we would reminisce about time spent with that sister, talking with her, laughing, going to a concert. Our time is always the most precious gift we can ever give.

In our family, Josh and I always give each other planned date nights. We give our kids coupons for one-on-one time with us. Our kids give their close friends gift certificates for movie nights and sleepovers. How could you give your time—truly, your most precious resource—to someone you love?

In Brief

Gifts may seem like tricky terrain for minimalists, but they do not have to be. By opening conversations with your loved ones, remembering to always keep the love, and giving creative, meaningful gifts, you can enjoy many happy, clutter-free gift exchanges with your family and friends.

CHAPTER 14

One Last Thing Before You Go

Last summer I visited Wyoming and climbed three mountains. Before each climb, I stood at the bottom, looked up, and felt immediately intimidated by my distance from the top. But as I started to climb, I quit looking up as much and started looking down. Each time I stopped to catch my breath and survey my progress, I was amazed at how far I'd come.

Keeping my mind focused on what I'd already accomplished gave me the confidence to reach the top. And I did, each time.

Minimalism is a journey and we are all on different parts of the path, moving at our own individual pace. Each of us will reach our goal in our own way, in our own time. Some will take longer, and others will do it quickly. It doesn't matter.

What matters is that we keep climbing, one foot in front of the other, one drawer, cupboard, and closet at a time. Focus on how far you've come, the progress you are making, and you'll be amazed at how much easier it is to reach your goal.

Thank you for allowing me to share my minimalism journey with you. I hope this book has inspired you to seek the freedom that comes from living a life with less.

References

Carver, Courtney. "Project 333: Simple is the new black." Be More With Less. https://bemorewithless.com/project-333/. (accessed July 28, 2017).

Catalogue Choice. "Simplify Your Life: Stop Junk Mail for Good." https://www.catalogchoice.org/. (accessed July 28, 2017).

Daily Mail Reporter. "Lost Something Already Today? Misplaced Items Cost Us Ten Minutes a Day." DailyMail.com. http://www.dailymail.co.uk/news/article-2117987/Lost-today-Misplaced-items-cost-minutes-day.html. (accessed July 26, 2017).

Data and Marketing Association. Dmachoice.org. https://dmachoice.thedma.org/. (accessed July 28, 2017)

Drug Enforcement Administration. "National Prescription Drug Take Back Day." https://www.dea.gov/take-back/takeback-news.shtml. (accessed July 28, 2017).

Opt Out Services LLC. OptOutPrescreen.com. https://www.optoutprescreen.com/opt_form.cgi. (accessed July 28, 2017).

PaperKarma. The App To Stop Junk Mail. https://www.paperkarma.com/. (accessed July 28, 2017).

Story, Louise. "Anywhere the eye can see, it's likely to see an ad." The New York Times. http://www.nytimes.com/2007/01/15/business/media/15everywhere.html. (accessed July 26, 2017).

The Council for Textile Recycling. http://www.weardonaterecycle.org/. (accessed July 28, 2017).

Now What?

Want more minimizing inspiration? Of course you do!

Visit **RoseLounsbury.com** where you can:

- Register to receive some FREE bonus content! Rose's **Minimalism Starter Guide** will help you move past the overwhelm and create a personalized decluttering checklist so you can start creating more open spaces in your life today.

- Join Rose's FREE "Minimalism is Fun" Facebook group.

- Learn more about Rose's upcoming speaking events and online courses.

About the Author

After blogging about her personal journey toward minimalism, **Rose Lounsbury**—a former middle school English teacher—was inspired to help other women create more open spaces in their lives. She started a minimalism and simplicity coaching business in 2015 and has since helped hundreds of clients and students achieve stuff-free freedom. Rose spends her days writing, speaking, and teaching about minimalism, while soaking up the moments with her husband and their wild triplets in lovely Dayton, Ohio.

Rose is a regular guest on Fox News *Good Day Columbus* and has been featured on NPR, *Good Morning Cincinnati*, and *Living Dayton*. Her popular TEDx Dayton talk can be found on YouTube.

You can contact Rose by email at Rose@RoseLounsbury.com or visit her online at **RoseLounsbury.com**, where you can access her free resources and learn more about her upcoming speaking events and online courses.

Made in the USA
Columbia, SC
06 November 2023

25586243R00078